The View From My Front Porch

*a woman's approach
to developing a
Christian worldview*

Kay Harms

The View from My Front Porch
Published by Off the Beaten Path Ministries
Printed and distributed by Lulu.com

To order additional copies of this resource: order on line at www.offthebeatenpathministries.com.

Printed in the United States of America

Contents

About the Author

Born and raised in Georgia, author Kay Harms and her family now call Arizona home. She has been privileged to teach women's Bible studies and direct women's ministries at four different churches in three different states since she and her husband James entered the ministry in 1990.

Kay has a degree in journalism from the University of Georgia and writes for Christian magazines and devotional guides. She also speaks at women's events, serves as a MOPS mentor mom, and disciples teenaged girls.

Kay founded *Off the Beaten Path Ministries* as an avenue through which to teach God's Word to women and come alongside them on the narrow path, the one blazed by the ancient principles of the Bible. Kay's passion for studying God's Word was birthed when she attended a Precept Ministries training workshop in 1991. She has taught numerous Precept Bible study classes as well as other studies. A gifted teacher and discussion facilitator, Kay enjoys helping women discover the relevance of the Bible for their lives. She has authored several Bible studies and speaks at Bible conferences.

Raised in a strong Christian home, Kay loves the church and the opportunities she has had as a pastor's wife to minister up close and personally to women and families. She says one of the greatest blessings of her life in ministry has been the opportunity to "go backstage" and view some of God's greatest miracles as He has changed lives, rescued marriages, reunited parents with wayward children, and restored unity to fractured congregations.

Kay and James have two adult children, Daniel and Abigail, who keep them grounded and humble.

Thus says the Lord,
"Stand by the ways and see and ask for the ancient paths,
Where the good way is, and walk in it;
And you will find rest for your souls.

. . .

But they said, 'We will not walk in it.'
Jeremiah 6:16

Welcome to the Front Porch

When I was a child I loved playing on the porch. Whether it was the more formal front porch furnished with a simple black bench, the carport where I could roller skate when the cars were gone, or the screened-in back porch where I could swing or even relax on a twin-sized bed and read a favorite book, I loved the feel of being outside but still connected to my home, my safe place. From the porch I could hear the sounds of children playing, people driving by, birds singing, and neighborhood dogs barking, but I could also hear my mom cooking dinner, my brother watching television and my dad working on his latest project in the basement. I could experience the world, but with the safety of home still beneath my feet. Because I was just a child, there were times that the front porch was as far as I could get into my world. I may not have been allowed to venture down the street, but I could watch people come and go on that street from a distance. And I may not have been allowed to go into a neighbor's house, but I could watch those neighbors throw a Frisbee or weed the flower beds in their front yard. That porch was my window to the world. It provided a safe place from which I could view the world beyond me and my family.

You can imagine that my view of the world from the safety of my porch was rather limited. When I looked out from my front porch I simply saw other homes similar to mine. I saw well-tended yards that nevertheless showed a little wear and tear from the play of children and the antics of restless dogs. I saw seemingly happy moms and dads coming home from work, unloading bags of groceries, getting the mail, and mowing the grass. I saw suitably dressed, healthy and cared for children riding their bikes, bouncing balls, and jumping rope. I didn't see poverty, child abuse, neglect, or crime. I also didn't see affluence, extravagance, or high fashion. In fact I also rarely saw skin colors different from my own, and I never heard an unfamiliar language being spoken. My view of the world was very narrow, very short-sighted.

Obviously I get out a little more than I did as a child. Like you, I've been into a few homes that aren't just like mine. I've met people from different backgrounds, traveled to faraway places, lived on a diverse college campus, moved across country, and studied other cultures. I'm a fairly educated woman who reads voraciously, watches the evening news, flies to different cities several times a year, and surfs the Internet most every week. Still, unless I make a conscious effort to see things from the perspective of someone else, I tend to see my world from a very limited perspective, my perspective. No I don't just gauge my world based on the view from my front porch, but I do admit to seeing things from a limited vantage point.

If I'm honest I must admit my view of the world is based largely on what I have seen with my own eyes, my experiences, what I've read and heard from others, and even how I wish for things to be. Of course, as a follower of Jesus Christ I also like to think my view of the world finds its foundation in the words of the Bible. But while I've tried very hard to build my own personal life on the precepts of God's Word, I'm not sure I've been as conscientious about building my worldview upon those same truths. What about you? Do you have a completely biblical worldview?

Maybe I should back up a step or two. Perhaps I should first ask if you are aware that you have a worldview. Do you know what a worldview is? Before I began researching for this study I was blissfully ignorant about worldviews. I assumed philosophy professors, politicians and a few other movers and shakers probably had a set worldview, but I never realized that I indeed already had one too, whether I could give it labels and descriptions or not. Turns out, we all already have a worldview, even if we have never put much thought or effort into shaping it correctly. And most of us haven't.

Just like we all see our physical world from different viewpoints when we walk out onto the front porches of our homes, we also see the rest of our world from varying perspectives as well. We see the political landscape, the economy, and the culture around us differently. We look out at our world with different values, goals, morals, ideals, and priorities. We make decisions, handle money, navigate relationships, and deal with life's crises and successes in various ways.

The way we individually interpret and explain the world is the foundation of what is called our "worldview." The other part of our worldview is how we apply this interpretation to our life. We all look out from the front porches of our individual lives and view the world from a certain perspective. And as we stand on those "porches" and survey the world we make assessments that eventually affect the choices we make, the words we say, the opinions we espouse, and the goals we set. And, just like the location of my home determines the view from my front porch, there are factors that contribute to our worldviews. Our views of the world are influenced by our family life, our experiences, the things we have been taught, the things we've read or heard, the other people in our life, and so much more.

If you think this is just pie in the sky philosophy and not really relevant to you, think again. You see your worldview is what guides the choices you make every day. Your worldview answers for you the following questions and more:

- Is it okay for a woman to get an abortion if she was raped?
- How should I choose who to vote for in the next election?
- Is it okay for a Christian to marry a person of another faith?
- Should I take my neighbor to court if he refuses to trim the branches of his trees that hang over my yard?
- Are all religions just personal preferences that eventually lead to the same God?

> *"And, just like the location of my home determines the view from my front porch, there are factors that contribute to our worldviews."*

- Is it okay to get a divorce if you're no longer in love and you both agree it would be best to go in different directions?
- Is it best to have a sexual relationship with your partner before you get married so you can see if you're compatible?
- Should I keep quiet about my faith in the work place so as not to offend anyone?
- Are there some offenses that don't need to be forgiven?
- Should homosexual relationships be sanctioned as marriages?
- Are we responsible to help people suffering in other countries?
- Is *The Secret* really the key to happier, more successful living?

If I have a Christian worldview I will draw my answers to the above questions straight from God's Word, the Bible. If I do not have a Christian worldview, I may pull some of my answers from the Bible, but I will allow other factors to influence my decisions as well. Essentially a Christian worldview is one that looks at the world from God's perspective and responds to the world according to His authoritative Word.

But let's face it, because we've spent so much time rubbing shoulders with the world and because we hear the voices of so many different worldviews every day, few of us believers really cling to a Christian worldview in every area of life. Others assert their views so boldly and with such savvy. They sound so wise and sophisticated in their thinking. And they make those with a Christian worldview seem ill-informed, simple, close-minded, uneducated, and even hateful. In other words, their front porch looks like it has a much broader view, while ours is narrow and limited. Wouldn't it be better to see the world from such an expansive perch? Not necessarily.

Paul G. Hiebert, a missions anthropologist, suggests that while changes in *beliefs* and *behavior* have long been accepted as sufficient proof of one's conversion to Christianity, a third change is actually required to indicate genuine salvation. Hiebert says that true born-again believers will also, with time and discipleship, develop a Christian worldview that stands firm against the voices of this world. I agree with him. If I claim to have accepted the salvation offered through Jesus' death on the cross and have made Him the Lord of my life, then I should view the world from His perspective. And I should allow the truth of His Word to trump every other voice that claims to know what is true, best, or wise. Otherwise I have not completely put my trust in Him as my authority.

About This Bible Study

The purpose of this study is not to shame us for having adopted beliefs and values that contradict the Bible. Shame rarely produces positive results. Instead, we'll simply try to examine our current worldview, consider what an accurate Christian worldview consists of, and try to get our view of the world more in focus with the God of the Bible. To do this we'll:

- determine what factors have contributed to the formation of our current worldview
- reframe our worldview with two foundational building blocks
- take a fresh look at our world from our reconstructed "front porches"
- and, finally, examine the unique lives of women from that same front porch, the one with a biblical foundation.

How it Will Work

This brief study will require a lot of honest thought and intentional change on our parts. You can certainly do this study on your own, but you will probably have more success completing the study and gaining insight from it if you join at least a few other ladies for accountability and discussion on a weekly basis. For four weeks you will be asked to complete five days of Bible study each week. Some days may be a little more intense than others, but overall the assignments should take you less than 45 minutes. Still I encourage you to do a little bit each day. Don't try to cram it all in the day before you meet with your group for discussion. Let the scriptures you read sink in. Give yourself time to digest them. That way when you all get together, you will have had time to internalize the things you will address as a group.

Reading on My Front Porch

Each day we'll begin by spending some time just "sitting on our front porches" and reading from God's Word. Whether your front porch offers a rocking chair, a swing, or a few steps to sit on, take a seat and open the Bible to the specified passage for a view from God's Word. (Of course you don't actually have to sit on your front porch – mine is nothing more than a stoop. I'll sit in my living room, thank you very much. If the weather's just right, as it often is here in Arizona, I'll head out to my *back* porch.)

Visiting on My Front Porch

In this section of your daily assignment we'll discuss what we've read from the Scripture, where it hits us in our culture, how it needs to be applied, and any difficulties we have with what we've discovered. This will be our chance to get transparently honest about some things, do a little self-examination, and dialogue about the issues we encounter. We'll sit and have a friendly woman to woman chat about the truths we have been confronted with from God's Word.

Looking Out from My Front Porch

Not only do we need to uncover the roots of our own worldview, but we need to look at some of the more common worldviews held by those around us. We'll see how these views collide with each other and with the Bible. But we won't use this opportunity to look down on our world. Instead we want to look at our culture as a mission field that needs the Truth. So we'll use this time to develop a sensitivity and compassion for our world. We'll also occasionally do a little work on our own "front porches" or perspectives in this section, reframing the structure from which we view our world.

Leaving My Front Porch

As we leave our front porches each day we'll take a moment to pray. We'll ask for wisdom, clarity, guidance, and conviction. We'll confess our wrong thinking and ask God to help us correct it so our view of the world lines up with His. Finally we'll pray for our world and those who need Jesus.

Optional Discussion Questions

You'll find optional questions for discussion at the end of each week's assignments. If you're meeting with a group you'll have the opportunity to dialogue over these questions with other women who have been doing the same assignments you have. Hopefully you will gain something from each other's input. You may want to look over the questions before you meet and jot down a few ideas.

If you are doing the study solo, I encourage you to spend some time in personal reflection with these discussion questions the day after you have completed the final assignment for that week. This will give you the opportunity to recall what we learned throughout the week and make some further applications. It will work as a review and help you further nail down any new or challenging concepts.

Why This is Important

Developing a Christian worldview is crucial to living an obedient and abundant life in Christ Jesus. We need to *own* Christian worldviews we can pass down to the next generations. It may be the one thing they have to hold on to as our world becomes a darker place to live in the future.

I've often told my children that the one thing no one can take from you or force you to compromise on is your attitude. They can take your voice, your ability to move or act, your strength, your health, and even your life. They can change your circumstances, your location, and your future. But only you can determine your attitude. A Christian worldview is essentially the same thing as an attitude. It is the way we see things, act toward them, and respond because of them. And if our worldview has deep roots in the character of the one true God and His Word, then it will not be shaken when all else is.

Week 1 – My Vantage Point

It was Socrates who said that the unexamined life is not worth living. To examine one's life is to think about it. It is to evaluate. To evaluate requires examining values and value systems. We all have values. We all have some viewpoint about what life is all about. We all have some perspective on the world we live in. We are not all philosophers but we all have a philosophy. Perhaps we haven't thought much about that philosophy, but one thing is certain—we live it out. How we live reveals our deepest convictions about life… The theories we live are the ones we really believe.

R.C. Sproul[1]

This week we'll look at a few examples in the Bible that show us how easy it is to develop a worldview contrary to God's view of the world unless we are aware and alert. We'll identify some of the roadblocks that stand in our way to a biblical worldview and discover how to overcome those barriers.

Day 1 – Right in Whose Eyes?

Reading on My Front Porch
Read: Judges 17:1-13 in your Bible. Write verse 6 in the space below.

In those days there were no king in Israel; every man did what was right in his own eyes.

Visiting on My Front Porch
The verse you recorded in the space above is crucial to understanding Judges 17. In fact it is one of the key verses for accurately interpreting the whole book of Judges. Over and over the people of Israel got themselves into trouble by doing "what was right in their own eyes." They disregarded what God called right and wrong, and simply relied on their own flawed judgment to make decisions, enter into agreements, relate to other nations, and even worship.

In *Vines' Expository Dictionary of Old and New Testament Words*, the term "in their own eyes" is defined as *in their own opinion or view*. So the people were doing what they *viewed* to be right, but they weren't basing their *opinion* on any particular standard or guideline. We would say in current vernacular they were winging it. While we may be able to read Judges 17 and immediately detect some of the mistakes they were making, we may not be able to detect our own flawed thinking with such ease. After years of doing what we *perceive* to be right or acceptable, we may have become so accustomed to our own judgments that we don't even bother to assess them by a biblical standard, much less recognize them to be ungodly.

What are some examples in chapter 17 of people doing what was right in their own eyes?
Micah took his own levite as his own priest.
_____

_____

Why would it be wrong simply to do what is right in your own eyes? Why can't we all just decide what is best for ourselves in any given situation? Honor God by asking Him what to do. what is His plan for the situation I'm in?

_____

Many worldviews are developed largely by what people see with their "own eyes." If a person sees something often enough they become accustomed to it, accepting of it. Eventually, with enough exposure, what they have seen with their own eyes becomes the standard or even desirable. Even if something was deemed unacceptable or immoral in the past, with enough visibility that thing can become commonplace and normal. Before you know it that behavior, concept or attitude is considered to be right, just, best, and even godly.

What are some of the things in life that you have seen a lot of? What have you *personally* been exposed to repeatedly to the point that it has become commonplace? _____

_____

_____

What are some of the things in our culture that once were considered immoral or questionable but now seem commonplace and acceptable simply because we've seen so much of it? _____

_____

_____

_____

Looking Out From My Front Porch
When a nation or culture chooses to base its sense of rightness on what the people perccive to be right or wrong, rather than on an established, immovable, and holy standard, that culture begins a speedy tumble down a slippery slope. The target for

righteousness constantly moves and the standard for excellence drops lower and lower. People judge what is right and wrong on a case by case basis (situational ethics) and that lack of consistency trains the next generation to believe that everything is relative, there are no absolutes.

Do you see evidence of such moral relativism in our culture today? _____

Explain: _____

_____

_____

What are some of the current cultural hot topics that seem to be up for debate because everyone "sees" them differently? I'll get you started…

abortion _____   _____

sex out of marriage _____   _____

_____   _____

_____   _____

Leaving My Front Porch
Ask God to help you evaluate honestly the viewpoints you have adopted. Allow Him to show you if any of those are based solely on what you see to be right in your own eyes. Pray that He will use this study to correct those views so they line up with His standard. I'll give you space to write your prayer out if you wish.

Day 2 – Why Then Has All This Happened to Us?

Reading on My Front Porch
Read: Judges 6:1-18 in your Bible. Write verse 12 in the space below.

Visiting on My Front Porch
As chapter 6 of Judges opens we find the Israelites under the oppressive brutality of Midian. For seven years the Midianites have been abusing the Israelites by joining with other neighboring peoples and destroying the crops that the Israelites had just planted, as well as destroying their livestock. God's people felt like they were outnumbered and

without recourse. The Midianites were mean-spirited, too. Notice they didn't come and steal the Israelites' produce; they destroyed it and left devastation in their wake.

Nevertheless, God still had His eye on Israel. While He allowed them to experience the harsh treatment of the neighboring nations as a form of discipline, He waited patiently for them to call out to Him. I imagine it was after one of Midian's annual pillaging visits to Israel that the people finally cried out in desperation to their God.

Summarize the message God sent through a prophet to Israel. You'll find His response in

Judges 6:7-10. _____

_____

_____

As we examine the next common mistake made when building a worldview, it is important to note that God was still on His throne, had a plan, and even explained to the Israelites why their world had turned upside down.

Indeed the Israelites had experienced seven years of extreme oppression and misfortune. Consider the effects that would be felt by our own country if the Mid-West were to experience seven years of pestilence or drought, shutting down America's breadbasket. We would probably begin to assume the worst with each passing year and wonder if we'd ever see prosperity again.

So when the angel of the Lord appears to Gideon, the youngest of Joash's sons, He finds him threshing wheat in the wine press, not out in the open where one would normally thresh wheat. Gideon is operating out of fear because he has known so much brutal and savage oppression from the Midianites for so many of his young years. As far as Gideon can tell, the world is a cruel place, his God has forgotten his people, and he is powerless to make a difference. Does Gideon's worldview sound familiar?

The angel of the Lord calls Gideon "O valiant warrior," but Gideon cannot wrap his brain around that title. He's no warrior; he's a coward hiding in the wine press. In fact, the Lord's appearance only sets off a pity party in Gideon. He begins to whine in the wine press! Not only does he question his ability to be a great warrior, but he questions whether or not God is still with the people of Israel (vs. 13). He's heard of God's exploits on behalf of His people, but he's not sure he believes them. He surely hasn't seen any for himself. He's only experienced oppression, hate, fear, and probably poverty and hunger. And those experiences, not his knowledge of God, have shaped his view of the world.

Read Gideon's response to the angel of the Lord in verse 13. Have you ever asked God

such questions? When and why? _____

_____

_____

If we are not intentional about forming a Christian worldview based on the truth of God's character and His Word, we will follow in Gideon's path. We will naturally form our view of the world based on our own history. We'll look at the world through wounded eyes, fresh tears, haunting disappointments, and shattered dreams, and presume that no loving God could have possibly have been on His throne during our struggles and pain.

Think about your own history – your family experiences, education, relationships, health issues, hurts, and victories. What are some of the most significant things that come to mind? In other words, which experiences have had the most impact in shaping you and the way you see things?

_____

_____

_____

Not only did Gideon base his assessment of the world and his place in it on his *past* experience; he also drew his conclusions about God, himself, and his world from his *current* circumstances. We can admit that things looked bleak for Gideon and Israel. Surely he wasn't wrong to form his opinions based on what he was enduring at that moment. Or was he? What do you think?

_____

_____

_____

_____

Take a quick assessment of your current circumstances. What's going on in your personal life, family, work place, country, or world that could influence how you see the world?

_____

_____

_____

_____

_____

Looking Out From My Front Porch

Today we're not going to just look "out" from our front porch; we're going to look "up" from it. Quickly reread Judges 6:1-10. According to these verses, why were the people of Israel under the heavy hand of Midian? (Check all that apply)

- ○ It was just bad luck.
- ○ Israel had been disobedient to God.
- ○ God sought to bring Israel low.
- ○ The Midianites were wiser than Israel.
- ○ The Midianites ruled the world.
- ○ God was waiting for Israel to call out to Him.

Gideon may have felt like God had abandoned Israel, but He never had. In fact Israel had abandoned God and yet God continued to watch over them, listen for their call, and hasten to them when they did cry out. God was always in control of the situation, even though it must have seemed otherwise to Gideon and his fellow Israelites.

Of the things you listed in the previous section that you have experienced or are experiencing, which of them caused you to question where God was? List them in the left hand column on the next page.

My Experiences   Where Was God? What Was He
                                            Doing?

_____   _____

_____   _____

_____   _____

_____   _____

_____   _____

_____   _____

Now, in the column on the right I want you to jot down your thoughts on what you think God may have been doing or is doing now in each of those situations. If, after prayerfully thinking about it, you can't answer that question for one of your experiences, humbly write "I want to know" and give God time to gently show you what He was or is up to. You may not get the answer anytime soon, but someday, maybe in eternity, God will make it very clear to you that He was there all along.

Dear friends, more than anything today, I want us all to understand that sometimes we are quick to make judgments about the world when we sense that God is absent from a particular experience or circumstance. We figure God is not here, so I'll just make this call on my own. I don't see God in the situation, so I'll call the shots based on what I do see and what is clear to me. Not only is this dangerous and foolish; it's arrogant. For God, while not always immediately visible, is always there. He's there and He's at work.

Leaving My Front Porch

If you have experiences in the past or in the present that are causing you to doubt the stability, faithfulness, strength, or love of God, admit that to Him today. Ask Him to make His presence known to you today. Ask for just a glimpse into what He is doing and expect Him to show you. Thank Him for never leaving you and for always working on your behalf.

Day 3 – A Bad Report

Reading on My Front Porch

Read: Numbers 13:1-2 & 13:17 - 14:10 in your Bible. According to 13:32, what did the spies give to the sons of Israel? Write your answer in the space below.

Visiting on My Front Porch

Here again we see an example of someone basing their view of things on what they see with their own eyes. God has told Moses to send twelve men in to spy out the land of Canaan before He takes the nation in to conquer it for them. Keep in mind that God has miraculously delivered Israel from the bondage of Egypt, faithfully provided food and water for Israel, guided them to this land by His very presence, and protected them from their enemies. He has a proven track record with these people and now He has simply instructed them to go in and get a feel for things.

They got a feel for things alright. The twelve men saw the abundance of the land, but they also saw large and fortified cities, strong people, and descendants of their enemies. In the eyes of 10 of these men, the barriers to success far outweighed the benefits of moving in. They gave a *bad report* based on what they had seen during a 40-day scouting mission.

We've already learned the danger of developing our view of things based on what we see with our eyes. I'd like for us to focus on another danger that is so well-illustrated in this sad story. The Israelites as a whole, the people of this nation chosen and protected by the one true God, took the word of ten doomsayers over the word of two God-fearing, wise and courageous men. They believed a bad report simply because the majority gave it. The bigger mistake is that they simply disregarded the word of God on this issue. Reread Numbers 13:2. What did God say in regard to the land and the people of Israel?

O He might give them the land if they were lucky.

O He would let them have the land if they could defeat the enemies living in it.

O He would give the land to Israel.

O Israel would need to pay Him for the land.

God had already promised to give Israel the land, but now they were taking it upon themselves to decide whether or not to enter the land based on a bad report. The people believed the viewpoint of a few select men (chosen I'm sure based upon some noble characteristics), rather than the word of their God. Can you relate?

The spies acted as gatekeepers. They gave the Israelite people and Moses information they could not get for themselves. Moses and the masses could only see Canaan from a distance. They had limited information from their vantage point and were dependent on these twelve men to give them an accurate report of that which they could not see or experience. The twelve spies had been entrusted with the job of bringing back an accurate report, but instead they returned with opinions based on limited exposure, partial information and fear. Likewise, we have gatekeepers in our world who we trust to give us accurate information. We "appoint" them to their posts because they are supposedly knowledgeable, trustworthy, wise, expertly trained, impartial, and/or reliable. But, just like the twelve spies sent in to scope out the Promised Land, our gatekeepers often fail us.

The twelve spies used some tactics that should strike a note of familiarity with us as well. They kept the people away from the truth (1) by expressing their opinions loudly and forcefully. Numbers 13:31 infers that the gatekeepers with the bad report interrupted Caleb's attempt to quiet the people and reassure them. They insisted on being the experts. They also drove their message home (2) with substantial "facts" to back up their reasoning. They named names, nations, and places on the map, giving their report a sense of authority. Of course, upon closer examination, one would find these to be empty facts, inconsequential in comparison to the promises made by God. These gatekeepers also persuaded the people to listen to them by use of (3) exaggeration. They used phrases like "a land that devours its inhabitants" and "we became like grasshoppers in our own sight." Finally, they virtually sounded an alarm with their report by (4) invoking fear in the people. They left the Israelites no room to think through the information they gave them, but pushed them into compliance with their extreme opinions by scaring them to death. And by the time they were through giving their bad report, the people were no longer even willing to listen to Caleb and Joshua, the only two who still looked at things from God's perspective.

Who are some of the gatekeepers in our world? Who gives you reports (good or bad) about the things going on in our world? Who tells you how to look at things?

_____

_____

_____

On a scale from 1 to 10, 1 being none at all and 10 being complete, how much influence do you think these gatekeepers have on the worldviews of *most people*?

_____

1   5   10

On the same scale, how much influence do you think these gatekeepers have on *your* worldview? (Think about it and be honest.)

_____

1   5   10

Looking Out From My Front Porch

God told Moses to send in twelve spies to survey Canaan. He surely knew what they would see and, knowing the minds and hearts of men as He does, He undoubtedly knew that most of them would bring back an overwhelmingly bad report. I'm sure the bad report angered Him, but it appears from Numbers 14:11-12 that His anger was ignited more by the people's *response* to the report. I believe He desired for the people to weigh out what they heard, but not to give it more weight than it deserved. Surely He expected them to remember what He had said and done and promised, and to give those things the final authority and the most weight. Don't you suppose He expects the same of His children today?

Let's clarify one important thing. The report was not just bad because the ten spies gave *bad news*. The report was bad because *it contradicted what God had told them*. In fact, the report was probably mostly accurate, though a little exaggerated. But because they gave the report in a way that frightened and alarmed the people, the report caused the people to choose to ignore God's promises, His character, and His track record. *Any time we listen to information, whether it is based on fact or not, and then choose to give that information more weight than God's Word, we have succumbed to a bad report.* Even if a report contains seemingly good news but contradicts God's Word, that report is bad and should not be heeded.

How hard is it for you to watch the evening news or read the newspaper and sift through what you see and hear? Is it difficult to hold on to what God says is true when the "bad report" seems so substantiated and accurate? Tell me about it:

_____

_____

_____

Which of the following elements of a report (good or bad) from a gatekeeper make it hard for you to cling to what you know to be true from God's Word? In other words, which have the most power of persuasion with you? (Check as many as three)

O   Scientific evidence

O   Testimony of personal experience

O   Emotional appeal

O   Fear factors

O   Exaggeration

O   Urgency

O   Forceful and dogmatic pleas

O   Majority agreement (10 out of 12 spies, for instance)

O   Visual evidence such as video footage

O   other _____

What are some of the "bad reports" you have heard recently? Keep this question in mind for the rest of the week and jot down your answer as you hear any additional "bad reports." ("Bad reports" are not necessarily bad news. A "bad report" is anything presented as true and accurate that contradicts God's Word.)

Report: _____   Gatekeeper Who Reported It:

_____   _____

_____   _____

_____   _____

_____   _____

_____   _____

_____   _____

_____   _____

Leaving My Front Porch
Ask God to help you be aware of the gatekeepers and the reports they give. Grant God the freedom to point out to you bad reports and how those reports may have shaped your worldview. Ask Him to begin replacing those bad reports with truth. Only He can do that.

Day 4 – That's Not Fair

Reading on My Front Porch

Read: Numbers 14:26-45 in your Bible. What did Moses tell the people in verse 42? Write your answer in the space below.

Visiting on My Front Porch

Yesterday we learned how a bad report taken seriously caused the people to develop a view of their situation that was not accurate. In the end, the people found out that if you choose to look at things differently than God does, He'll let you have your own way to your own demise. We are wise to learn the same lesson from their mistake.

Today I want to consider one more obstacle that prevents us from having an accurate and biblical view of our world. See if you agree with me on this.

I have found that when I try to make everything in the world fair and equitable I end up discounting the truths found in the Bible. God has given me truth in His Word and it is nothing but truth. There may be things in the Bible that do not make sense to me or that I don't comprehend as fair, but it is still truth. I simply have to trust that my God is far wiser and smarter than I am and He will reveal the why's and how's in His good time. Meanwhile, it is my job to trust Him.

When I take the situations of this world and try to make them fair in my eyes, I tread on dangerous ice. You see, because of our sin, we live in an imperfect and fallen world. This world does not operate the way God intended it to originally. He put man and woman in a perfect, lovely, harmless, and balanced environment. They were in complete harmony with each other and perfect relationship with Him. Created in His image, Adam and Eve were given a free will. They had options. They were not robots without the ability to choose their own course. They could choose to follow God's instructions or they could willfully go their own way. We find the results of their first bad choice in Romans 5:12. Read this verse in your Bible and fill in the blanks with the appropriate words.

Therefore, just as through one man _____ entered the world, and _____

through sin, and so death spread to _____ _____ because all

_____.   Romans 5:12 (NASB)

We live with the results of that initial sin. But lest we think our crazy world can all be blamed on Adam, consider the final part of Romans 5:12. We are all born with a propensity to sin. Romans 3:23 also reminds us that we *all* sin and fall short of God's holy standards. Now we live in a world where we people do dreadful things, we have perverse thoughts, we have inordinate cravings and lusts, we lack self-control, we act selfishly and hurtfully, and we eventually die. While thankfully God has already set into motion a plan to redeem the world to Himself through the life and death of Jesus Christ, that which is yet redeemed is still unable to live in a way that produces peace and harmony. Therefore, the moral climate of our world continues to worsen instead of improve.

According to Romans 8:7-8 why does mankind continue to seem more and more

depraved, rather than more gentle, kind, peaceable, and loving?_____

As long as unredeemed men and women walk on this earth there will be evil, unrest, strife, and depravity. But not only are the people of this world affected by the evil inherent in our fleshly disposition; nature also suffers the consequences of man's fall. Romans 8:20 says the earth was "subjected to futility." The Greek word interpreted *futility* here means "spoiled, unable to fulfill its original purpose." No, the earth is not operating the way God created it to. Instead of thriving harmony we have decay, destruction, and disease. The earth itself groans from our sin and the results are natural disasters that threaten and destroy the lives of innocent people. Sickness ends most lives and violence, accidents, and unexplainable misfortune claim others. No, there is no fairness in the world we live in. To check out the validity of what I'm saying, read Romans 8:18-22. Fill in the following blanks.

Romans 8:20 says creation was subjected to _____.

Romans 8:21 says creation will one day be set free from its slavery to_____.

Romans 8:22 says the whole creation _____ and _____the

pains of childbirth.

One consequence of man's sin is that all is not right in the world. When a woman accepts that fact, realizes that her own sin keeps her separated from God and His goodness, and bows the knee before Him, she finds grace and mercy in the form of our Savior, Jesus Christ. There at the cross where He died for us, she finds forgiveness, restoration, life, and the promise of a better day. But, on the contrary, when a person tries stubbornly to manipulate fairness in a fallen world, she misses the grace of God and finds judgment instead. Our passage in Numbers 14 illustrates that perfectly.

The people of Israel found themselves suffering the consequences of defying and not trusting God. They were told they would not enter the Promised Land, but would instead die in the wilderness. The next generation would be able to enter the land with Joshua and Caleb, the two spies who brought back a good report, a God honoring report. While this news caused the children of Israel to mourn greatly (vs. 39), it doesn't appear their mourning was over their sin, but over the consequences. If you have children who have ever been punished for their wrongdoing and cried because they hated the punishment, you can identify. This wasn't genuine, humble repentance. Basically, they were crying, "That's not fair!"

The next morning the Israelites decided they would make what didn't seem fair in their minds more equitable. They would simply retrace their steps, pretend like nothing had ever happened and go into the land after all. Surely God would take back His harsh discipline. That would only be fair! They assumed God would give them the land after all. Big mistake. God was no longer in this thing. He had justly and righteously removed Himself from this endeavor. Verse 44 tells us the people "went up *heedlessly* to the ridge of the hill country" (italics mine for emphasis). That means they didn't heed God's just punishment, they disregarded Moses' warnings, and they took matters into their own hands. As predicted, God wasn't with them and they were defeated.

Looking Out From My Front Porch

I am afraid you may not be following me at this point (praise the Lord if you are!) so I'm going to make a few clear applications. Consider the following list of controversial topics. Many people would claim that God's estimation of these practices do not *seem* fair. They believe the Bible must be faulty or that Christians are misinterpreting the Bible's position on these practices. Think about why they don't seem fair and jot your thoughts down in the available space. (Don't feel bad for claiming that some of these things don't seem fair; at first glance I think some of them don't too.) Then see if you can identify some of the ways our culture has tried to make them fair by manipulation. What are some of the views that have been adopted in order to legitimize what God has called sin? (I'll get you started with some thoughts on the first one.)

Homosexuality – Shouldn't two people be able to be together legitimately if they love each other? If some people say they truly desire a lover of the same sex, who are we to say that is wrong? Especially if they say they've always felt that way?
Our culture has said people are born that way, so it's ok. Our culture has said it's a legitimate sexual orientation.

Prostitution

Divorce

Abortion

Each of these topics is clearly addressed in God's Word. He has given us the truth in each instance. Sometimes the truth He's given us, quite honestly, doesn't *seem* totally fair. Still, His is the final word. When we develop a worldview based on our idea of fairness instead of God's Word we do not have a Christian worldview. Period.

Leaving My Front Porch
Ask God to show you if you have allowed your desire for fairness to overrule your desire to honor Him in developing your worldview. I know I have. I want life to be fair. I want to be able to have a fair and equitable explanation for everything. But right now, things just aren't always fair. I have to bend the knee to God on that. Maybe you need to too.

Day 5 – Can't We All Be Friends?

Reading on My Front Porch
   Read: Deuteronomy 7:1-2; Judges 1:27 - 2:4 in your Bible. What did God tell the Israelites to do upon moving into the Promised Land that they did not do? Write your answer below.

Visiting on My Front Porch
   The Israelites have moved into the Promised Land to take possession. God has gone before them in battle and given them success over the nations the previous generation feared so greatly. The land is everything God promised it would be and they are home at last. Life is good. Except they have neglected to follow through with one assignment God gave them. They were to completely drive out the inhabitants of the land, but instead they are living among them. In some cases they are simply allowing the people of Canaan to live alongside them; in others they are using them as forced labor. Both scenarios are wrong. God is not pleased. He warns the people He will no longer do anything to drive out the enemies Himself and they will eventually become "as thorns in their sides."
   But why did God insist on Israel driving out the Canaanites to begin with? Couldn't they just co-exist? Couldn't they just all be friends? Quite simply, no. For further explanation, let's read an entry from the *Evangelical Commentary on the Bible*:

> The ancient curse on Canaan by Noah had been reiterated at Sinai. Moses now states it as a program of conquest and extermination, especially because of the degenerate nature of Canaanite religion. Their hatred of the Lord whose witness they had heard since the patriarchal period is now under the everlasting ban of extermination; as reprobates they are devoted to the wrath of God. Intermarriage is prohibited not for social reasons but for religious reasons as 7:4 makes clear: "for they will turn your sons away from following me to serve other gods." Positive consecration to the Lord demanded in chapter 6 calls for total destruction of pagan religious cults.[2]

God's command to drive out completely the inhabitants of Canaan was not some arbitrary decree made on a whim by a cruel god. It was both a just extermination of a repeatedly and historically wicked people and a safeguard for the covenant nation of Israel. God knew what He was doing, as He always does.

   Without me going any further, do you notice a correlation between Israel's neglect to drive out the enemies of God and the currently popular worldview of tolerance? Explain.

_____

_____

_____

   Let's see what the Bible has to say about how we are supposed to view philosophies, religions, and people that oppose God and His Word. Read the following scriptures in your Bible and jot down a summarizing statement for each in the space provided.

Romans 12:2   _____

                                     _____

2 Corinthians 6:14-18   _____

                                     _____

1 John 2:15-17   _____

                                     _____

Just so we're on the same page, here are the bottom line summaries of these scriptures:

1. Do not become like the world (the unredeemed).

2. Do not be bound together with unbelievers in marriage or other partnerships.

3. Do not love the things of the world or develop a taste for its pursuits.

I would summarize all three of these with one explicit command: *Put healthy boundaries in place.*

Do these scriptures sound cruel to you, excessive, or unfriendly? (Circle one)

yes   no   a little   maybe   I'm not sure

Even if these directives from God do sound extreme, are you willing to bend the knee and obey them because you realize they come from a just God who has your best interest at heart?

absolutely   no way   with some prayer   most of the
                                                                                       time

Please understand that these passages do not tell us to hate the people of the world or to treat them hatefully. In fact, the Bible tells us God so *loved* the world that He sent His Son to die for it. He still loves the *people* of this world and does not wish for anyone to perish. As His children and ambassadors, we are to love the people of this world as well. We are to show compassion to them, tell them the good news of Jesus Christ, and treat them with godly character.

But we also must realize that Satan, the prince of this world, holds much of this world in his web of deception. The world systems, philosophies, religions, pursuits, ideologies, and values are of his device. *They* are tools of the enemy and we must steer completely clear of them, just as the Israelites were to rid their land of the Canaanites.

Looking Out From My Front Porch

One of the greatest hindrances to developing a biblical worldview is our desire not to offend anyone. Most of us want to be liked. We want to "get along." We're taught from an early age to be polite, inoffensive, likeable, and easy going, as we should be. But God makes no bones about the fact that the gospel is offensive to many who refuse to humble themselves. He also contends that if the world dislikes Jesus and finds Him annoying, offensive, intolerant, and narrow-minded, then they will also find His true followers to be likewise. We must decide if we are willing to be associated with Jesus and His teachings or if we would rather enjoy a friendship with this world.

Read Matthew 13:57, Matthew 15:10-12 and 1 Peter 2:6-8. How do these verses describe

Jesus?

___easy going   ___offensive   ___likeable   ___popular

Now read Matthew 10:22, Matthew 24:9, John 15:19, and John 17:14. According to Jesus, what will the world do to those who adhere to a strict interpretation of the Bible and identify themselves with Jesus?

___love them   ___understand them   ___hate them   ___kill them

Leaving My Front Porch

Dear friends, a biblical worldview is going to be judged offensive by the world. We have to decide if we are willing to be seen as intolerant, close-minded, foolish, uneducated, unsophisticated and unkind. It's not that we *want* to be seen that way, but we *will be* viewed as such if we truly embrace a biblical worldview. On the other hand, if you desire friendship with the world more than you desire to please God, you will not be able to hold on to a true biblical worldview. I know we've read a lot of Scripture today, but I'd like you to read one more passage before we close. Read this passage and allow it to speak afresh to you. Then, in your prayer, express to God how you feel about this dilemma, ask Him whatever you may need to, and make any commitment you are able to make.

Please read John 12:42-43 and respond in prayer.

---

[1] R. C. Sproul, *Lifeviews* (Fleming H. Revell, 1986), 25.
[2] Walter A. Elwell, Evangelical Commentary on the Bible (Grand Rapids: Baker Book House, 1989), 116.

Discussion Questions

1. Make a list of the cultural hot topics that are up for debate because everyone "sees" them differently.

2. Why did Gideon have such a hard time seeing things from God's perspective?

3. What are some of the things you have experienced, either firsthand or secondhand, that get in the way of you having a biblical worldview? In other words, what are some of the worldly "causes" that you are sympathetic to simply because you have wrestled with that situation yourself or you know someone who has?

4. Talk about who the gatekeepers are. List them.

5. Have you heard any "reports" lately that caused you to do a double take? Any reports that didn't seem to check out with God's Word? (Danger: don't spend too much time on this question! Make sure you get to the last three; then you can return to this one if needed.)

6. What are some of the ways gatekeepers give "bad reports" besides reporting that which is in stark contrast to God's authoritative Word?

7. Discuss "Looking Out From My Front Porch" on Day 4.

8. Why does our desire to be liked by others get in our way of developing a biblical worldview? How can we reconcile these two desires – to be liked and to be godly?

Week 2 – A Change In Perspective

"Unfortunately, Christians have all too often neglected the command to love God with our minds, not just our hearts. This often is a result of having emphasized feeling over thinking. We need to learn to think biblically and to have the integrity to live out what the Bible teaches, since the Bible alone provides a true, livable worldview."[1]

Rick Warren & Charles Colson

Day 1 – Let's Start at the Very Beginning

Reading on My Front Porch

Read: Proverbs 1:7 in your Bible. According to this verse, what is the first thing needed to see the world the way God does? Now read Job 28:12-28.

Visiting on My Front Porch

The knowledge spoken of in Proverbs 1:7 is the Hebrew word da'at, a noun formed from the Hebrew verb yādá, which means "to know by observing and … reflecting …experiencing …considering." It is an intimate, experiential knowledge. So in essence, Proverb 1:7 implies that a deep and experiential knowledge or understanding of this world *begins with fearing God.* My guess is that if you skip this initial step—fearing God—you can't really have a firm grasp on the world. In other words, if you don't fear God you'll never really know as much as you might think you do! Do you agree? Why or why not?

_____

_____

Our supporting scripture in Job 28:12-28 goes on to tell us that fearing God leads to wisdom and understanding. And Proverbs 9:10 says, "The fear of the Lord is the beginning of wisdom, and the knowledge of the Holy One is understanding." Once again we see that a healthy fear of the Lord is a prerequisite for knowledge or wisdom. So to build a biblical or Christian worldview we must begin with a fear of God.

What do you think it means to fear God? Check all the answers you believe are accurate.

- ○ To stand in awe of who God is.

- ○ To recognize the power and position of God.

- ○ To give God the proper and deserved respect because of who He is.

- ○ To stay up late at night wondering if God is going to cause you harm.

- ○ To submit to a proper relationship with God.

- ○ To run away from God.

- ○ To respect the superiority of God and give Him final say.

All of the above answers are correct except for the 4th and 6th definitions. A proper fear of God does not evoke distrust, skepticism, or skittishness. But those who fear God will honor, respect, listen to, obey, and trust God. Let's answer a few more questions about fearing God and, specifically, about your fear of God.

Do you fear God? (according to the correct definition of the word?) _____ yes _____ no

If you answered "yes," why do you fear God? _____

_____

If you answered "no," why do you not fear God? _____

_____

On a scale from 1 to 10, 1 being very little and 10 being completely, how much does your *life* indicate that you truly fear God? Does your behavior give evidence that you fear God?

_____

1   5   10

If knowledge begins with the fear of God, then the fear of God begins with knowledge. A knowledge of God, that is. When a person truly knows God (yādá – experientially, intimately, and reflectively knows God), that person will certainly have a healthy fear of God. In fact, scripture indicates, and Christians throughout the ages agree, that the more one gets to know God the more they fear Him. Once again, we're not talking about a skittish, frightful fear, but a reverential and obedient fear.

As you get to know your God through scripture and first-hand experience, you see how big He is, how powerful, how trustworthy, how authoritative, how wise, and how loving He is. While at first you may have bent the knee in submission to Him only because you felt you had no other choice, you eventually bend the knee to Him because you trust and love Him. You long to please Him and you respect His authority in your life. Not only that, but you trust His wisdom about everything pertaining to life. If He says you must forgive others as He has forgiven you (and He does say this!) then you choose to forgive even the most heinous offense because you trust His authority. You don't forgive because it's easy or common sense or good advice; you forgive because the God you fear says to. You know that He knows what He's doing and you trust Him enough to obey Him. That's fearing God.

Knowing the one true God, and thus fearing Him, is the first step in developing a biblical worldview. Let's think about that today. Here's the way I see it:

The First Key to Building a Biblical Worldview is:

1. Get to *know* the one true God.

2. Out of that knowledge, develop a healthy *fear* of God.

3. Gain *wisdom*, which is seeing the world the way

God sees it.

Looking Out From My Front Porch

As you look around your world do you see a healthy fear of God? Do you think most people fear God? Do you see evidence that people do not fear God? What are some of the evidences that people do fear God and what are some of the telltale signs that people do not fear Him? Write your responses in the spaces below.

Evidences in peoples' lives that show they *do fear God*:

_____

_____

_____

Evidences in peoples' lives that show they *do not fear God*

_____

_____

_____

Leaving My Front Porch

As we leave our front porches today, let's bend the knee before our God. I highly encourage you to physically bow before Him if you can. It does wonders for my attitude when I simply get on my knees before God, even if I ache and groan as I'm getting up! Tell God what you think of Him. And ask Him to help you know Him better so you can respond to Him correctly.

Day 2 – Getting to Know Him

Reading on My Front Porch

Read: 1 Chronicles 16:8-36 in your Bible. As you read, write down all the active verbs that are in the form of instructions. If you need a little review, verbs are words that *do* something. For instance, the first instruction/verb I see in my translation (NASB) is "give thanks" (vs. 8), the second is "call" (vs. 8), and the third is "make known" (vs. 8). Write the scripture numbers beside your verbs or verb phrases.

1 Chronicles 16:8-36 – Action Verb Instructions

Visiting on My Front Porch

I know that was a lot of work to begin the lesson with. I'll try to make the rest of it easier on you!

Yesterday we talked about the importance of 1) knowing God well so we can 2) fear Him with a healthy fear and 3) gain knowledge and wisdom about our world, thus building a biblical worldview. Just so we can all be on the same page, I'd like for you to fill in the blanks of the step-by-step outline below. If you need a little help you can take a peek at yesterday's lesson, but try to do it on your own.

The First Key to Building a Biblical Worldview is:

1.   Get to _____ the one true God.

2.   Out of that knowledge, develop a healthy _____ of God.

3.   Gain _____, which is seeing the world the way

        God sees it.

Now let's begin that process by getting to know our God. In the scripture you read today, 1 Chronicles 16:8-36, Asaph, the chief minister of praise appointed by David to continually provide praise before the Ark of the Covenant, acknowledges God with a beautiful psalm. You'll notice that he wrote many of the psalms we have in our Bible. The reason I had you read this particular one is because I believe it holds several keys for *getting to know God*. They are found in the action verb instructions you recorded as you read through the psalm. Why don't you look over those now and see if you notice any instructions that Asaph gave that would help you know God better?

I'll not give you these instructions in the order Asaph gives them, but in the order that I think they naturally occur in a growing relationship with God. Keep in mind that I'm assuming you have a relationship with God through Jesus Christ. If you don't, that's where you'll need to begin. But if you are a Christian and simply need to get to know your God better, here are the steps we find in Asaph's psalm:

1. **Seek the Lord**. (Vs. 8, 10, 11) Verse 8 tells us to "call upon His name" and verse 11 says to seek the Lord, His strength, and His face (His presence) continually. If I want to know my God, I must purposefully seek Him in prayer and Bible study. In prayer I should ask Him to reveal Himself to me, to make His presence known to me, and to speak to me. If I'm having a hard time "finding Him" in my prayer time, as is sometimes the case if we're all honest, I can always find Him in His Word. He's on every page. Psalm 119:38 says "Establish Thy word to Thy servant, as that which produces reverence for Thee."

2. **Ascribe to the Lord the glory due His name**. (Vs. 28, 29) To "ascribe" means "to attribute something to a specified cause, source, or origin; to consider that a particular quality is possessed by something or someone." To get to know God, find out what the Bible says about Him and then doggedly ascribe those attributes to Him. For instance, Psalm 46:1 says, "God is our refuge and strength, a very present help in trouble." I need to read this scripture, write it down, believe it and live like it's true. That's how I attribute faithfulness and strength to God, two qualities that are truly His. I can follow the same pattern to ascribe to the Lord that He is indeed my creator, my redeemer, and my avenger. I should also ascribe to Him such qualities as holy, righteous, merciful, trustworthy, loving, and good. If the Bible says God is a certain way, then He is. Period.

3. **Remember His wonderful deeds which He has done**. (Vs. 12, 15) To *know* God is to know Him experientially, having considered and examined His ways. As I seek Him in prayer and Bible study and accurately ascribe correct qualities to Him, I will begin to notice the things He is doing in my life. I will feel Him walking me through a difficult situation, see Him provide my needs, watch Him fight my battles, and hear Him give me direction. Not only do I need to notice His work in my life; I need to remember it, recount it. Especially when the world seems to be spinning out of control or things are not "adding up" I need to remember the wonderful deeds I have witnessed Him do.

4. **Worship the Lord**. (Vs. 8, 10, 23, 29, 30, 34) Not only do I need to accurately ascribe to Him those characteristics which are truly His, but I need to thank Him, praise Him and give Him a "shout out" for being those things. I need to acknowledge His worth and in doing so I will put Him on the throne where He rightly resides. When God is on His throne, and He always is, all is right in the world whether it seems that way or not.

5. **Speak of all His wonders**. (Vs. 8, 9, 23, 24) Perhaps one of the reasons Christians are struggling to maintain a biblical worldview is that we've become hesitant, even among ourselves, to talk about the God we know. As you get to know your God and you see Him working, providing, ruling, and moving in your midst, don't be silent about it. Tell others. Remind those around you about God's character, ways and Word.

Looking Out From My Front Porch

Today we've considered five ways to get to know our God so that we know Him deeply and fear Him respectfully. How well do you know God? Do you know a god of your own imagination or the one true God? Do you know the god the spiritual gurus talk about on popular talk shows or do you know the Jehovah God of the Bible? Do you know a god who is easily manipulated and dumbed down or do you know the omnipotent, omniscient, omnipresent Creator of the world? Do you know a Santa Clause in the sky who should be obligated to answer your every request as long as you're good or do you experientially know the self-existent, sovereign Abba Father who loves you enough to discipline you and occasionally say "no"? Do you know the true God? Whatever your knowledge of God, it is never too late to get to know Him better.

Under each directive write one or two specific ways you can apply that instruction to get to know God better. I'll get you started.

1. **Seek the Lord**.

   Read through the Bible. Have a daily quiet time with God.

2. **Ascribe to the Lord the glory due His name**.

3. **Remember His wonderful deeds which He has done**.

4. **Worship the Lord**.

5. **Speak of all His wonders**.

Leaving My Front Porch

Make today's closing prayer a pledge of commitment to get to know your God more intimately. Ask Him to reveal Himself to you as you actively seek Him. Ask Him to correct any misconceptions you have about His character or ways. Spend a few minutes remembering how He has ministered to you recently. Then worship Him and recognize His rightful place of authority in your life. And throughout the day, take advantage of every opportunity you have to boast about the God who is so good to you.

Day 3 – Ascribe to Him the Glory He is Due

Reading on My Front Porch

Read: Daniel 11:32 in your Bible. What does the Bible say that those who know their God will do?

Visiting on My Front Porch

Today we are simply going to spend some time getting to know our God. Specifically we will *seek Him* in His Word and *ascribe to Him* the appropriate characteristics. Once again, I'm convinced that when we become truly persuaded that God is who the Bible says He is we will fear Him, and our worldview will begin to take a biblical shape. However, that means you have to really believe that God is the God He says He is to your very core. So as we look at a variety of scriptures today that reveal God's character to us, let's prayerfully take this information in and allow it to sink into the deepest parts of our being. If you just have a real struggle swallowing some of these attributes of God, tell Him. And give Him the room and time to prove Himself to you. Our understanding of God can't be based on head knowledge alone. We must believe in His character to the point that it transforms our thinking and our behavior. As you examine these scriptures, ask yourself if you live in light of the godly character traits you unearth.

In your Bible, look up the scriptures listed in the left hand column on the next page. Draw a line matching the scripture to the characteristic of God that is described in that passage.

Scripture	Character Trait of God
Genesis 1:1	our refuge
Genesis 16:13, Proverbs 15:3	holy
Genesis 17:1	hears me
Exodus 15:26	sees all
Leviticus 19:2	Almighty (all sufficient)
Psalm 16:2	sovereign, in charge
Psalm 62:8	the only true God
Psalm 103:19	healer
Psalm 115:3	creator of heaven and earth
Psalm 116:1-2	accountable to no one
Psalm 118:1	provider
Isaiah 46:9	good
Philippians 4:19	Lord
1 John 4:16	love

Looking Out From My Front Porch

So many people in our culture have inaccurate ideas about God. They build their knowledge of God on other people's misconceptions and false statements. One misconception upon another they create a weak, careless, uninvolved, mean, or apathetic god – one who can be easily controlled, explained away, and dismissed. Friend, you don't want to know those gods and you certainly won't fear them (with a healthy fear). You want to know the one true God. And as you get to know Him, first from His Word and then from your experience with Him, you will find Him to be so worthy of your respect. Your knowledge of Him will change the way you see everything else and your worldview will line up with His Word.

Circle three of the attributes of God listed above that minister most to you today.

Put a star beside any of the attributes you realize could change the way you are currently looking at a cultural issue.

Leaving My Front Porch

Read Colossians 1:9-12. In these verses Paul is telling the people of Colossae what he prays for them – that they would know their God in ever increasing amounts. As you reread this passage, turn it into a prayer for yourself.

Day 4 – Do You Need A Root Job?

Reading on My Front Porch

Read: Luke 8:4-15 in your Bible. Look again at verse 13. Why does Jesus say these hear the word, receive it with joy, and yet fall away from the truth eventually?

Visiting on My Front Porch

The second foundational component for developing a biblical worldview is being firmly rooted in the Word of God. You see, if we're going to stand firm on anything it needs to be the Bible. Having a Christian worldview doesn't mean espousing Christian *opinions*; it means holding firm to Christian *doctrine*, and that is found only in the Bible. When I am deeply rooted in the Bible, I am able to discern truth from error, godly wisdom from human reasoning, and God's standard from man's opinion.

But if I'm going to be one of those "fanatics" who believe that the Bible is the authoritative truth, I need to be persuaded that it actually is 100% reliable. Is it? Let's find out.

Read 2 Timothy 3:16-17 in your Bible. According to this passage all Scripture is: (Check all that apply)

○ inspirational

○ inspired by God

○ useful or profitable

○ full of error

○ easy to read

○ fable

While much of Scripture is inspirational, much of it also is just plain convicting! And truthfully much of the Bible is not so easy to read. It takes the assistance of the indwelling Holy Spirit to truly understand God's Word and even then we can still be stumped by many passages. However, just because the Bible sometimes seems hard to understand, doesn't mean we should just give up and let the "professionals" handle it. God desires for us to learn to study His Word responsibly, using well established techniques and trustworthy study aids so we can apply it to our daily lives. And as we're studying and happen across the occasional difficult passage, we shouldn't assume the Bible contains mistakes or contradictions. Instead we must approach the Bible with humility and allow God the opportunity to teach us what we need to know. When I come across a passage that seems hard to grasp, I try to put it into perspective by remembering a simple little rhyme: The main things are the plain things and the plain things are the main things. God has made very plain the main things we need to study and apply. Rather than fretting over the difficult and controversial teachings, I need to get busy applying those teachings that are very plainly repeated throughout the Bible. In fact the entire Bible *is* inspired by God and useful to the one who reads it. What does it mean that "all Scripture is inspired by God"?

The Greek word from which we get the word "inspired" actually means "breathed." So the Word of God has been *breathed out* by God. You may know that the Bible is actually made up of 66 separate books penned by approximately 40 different authors over a period of 1,400 – 1,800 years. Many people don't understand how such a compilation could be attributed to a divine author, but 2 Timothy 3:16 answers that dilemma. The self-existent, omniscient, eternal Creator of this world *breathed* His divine message into the hearts and pens of each purposefully chosen writer. Just like the sun shines radiant light through the panes of a stained glass window casting illumination in a variety of colors, God spoke His true and accurate message through the various personalities and writing styles of approximately 40 different men. The stained glass window is simply the agent through which the originating source of light shines its colorful rays. In the same way, the "authors" of the 66 books of the Bible are simply the personalities and voices through which God breathed His authoritative Word. And in doing so He has given us a Bible complete with history, poetry, proverbs, prophecy, epistles or letters, and instruction, in language that resonates uniquely with every heart it enters. While the pens, or quills, may have changed from one hand to another down through the ages, the message continued to flow from the same heart – the heart of God. And for that reason, the message stayed consistent and true to God's character and purposes through all those years. Just how amazing and creative is that!

Read 2 Peter 1:20-21. According to this passage, who was the driving force in the writing

of the Bible? _____

We can trust the authority of scripture because, though men may have written it, the Bible came from the heart of God through the Holy Spirit. It is God's love letter to His people.

Still, many raise the question, "How do we know the Bible has been accurately translated and preserved over thousands of years?" Good question. If you take the time to study how our modern Bible was passed down over the generations by the careful work of scribes and Massoretes (Jews who meticulously copied the Old Testament books in the early 10th century through a painstaking system of counting letters and words for accuracy) you will be astounded at how the Bible measures up in authenticity compared to any other ancient text. The Bible is undoubtedly more authentic and accurate than the writings of Homer, Polybius, Herodotus, or Plutarch, all texts that are universally recognized as genuine and reliable.

Let's build the case for the Bible's authority a little more. There are four types of proofs of the Bible's reliability:

1. The <u>external</u> evidence says the Bible is a *historical* book. External evidences include original texts, archaeology, and history that align with the accounts in the Bible.

2. The <u>internal</u> evidence tells us the Bible is a *unique* book. Internal evidences include authors with eyewitness accounts, consistency within the Bible, and fulfilled prophecies.

3. The <u>personal</u> evidence says the Bible is a *powerful* book. Personal evidences include the fact that it has been translated into over 1,300 languages, there have been millions of lives changed by its supernatural words, it is the all-time bestseller, and people have loved it enough to painstakingly preserve it through the years.

4. <u>Jesus</u> said the Bible came from God. He quoted Old Testament scripture, affirmed the authorship of the Holy Spirit, assured the prophecies would be fulfilled, and called scripture "the word of God."

Personally, I believe the fact that Jesus affirmed scripture as being God's authoritative Word to be the most powerful evidence that it is trustworthy. One more way that Jesus ascribed authority to the Bible is that He affirmed the people, events, and places in the Bible as authentic. Look up the passages on the left and match them with the appropriate people and places affirmed by Jesus to be real.

Matthew 10:15   the Prophets

Matthew 12:40   Jonah & the fish

Matthew 19:4   Sodom & Gomorrah

Matthew 22:40; 24:15   Noah & the flood

Luke 17:26   Adam & Eve

Looking Out From My Front Porch

Dear friends, a strong case has been built for the integrity and authenticity of the Scriptures, even if I've only given you a few of the basic tenets of that case in today's lesson. If you still struggle with believing in the authority of God's Word as a reliable, historical, prophetical, and life-changing document, I encourage you to continue your study of Bible authenticity. However, the real purpose of today's lesson isn't just to convince you that the Bible is reliable, but to establish that the Bible is uniquely God's Word. It is our manual for living because it comes from the One who gave us life. No other book, philosophy or teaching has the power to change lives that the Bible has. It is, quite simply, truth. And believing that is what will set you apart from many people in our world.

Just to get a firm grasp on what you believe about the Bible, answer the following questions honestly.

1. Do you believe the Bible is completely trustworthy for answering every question in life?

_____yes   _____ no   _____ not sure

2. Do you believe the historical accounts of the Old Testament are true?

_____yes   _____ no   _____ not sure

3. Do you believe the miracles of the Old and New Testaments, of Jesus, and of the apostles really occurred?

_____yes   _____ no   _____ not sure

4. Do you believe you should give the Bible authority in your life, even though it was written centuries ago?

_____yes   _____ no   _____ not sure

5. Do you believe the prophecies concerning the second coming of Jesus and the end of the age are reliable?

_____yes   _____ no   _____ not sure

Leaving My Front Porch

As we leave our front porches today let's return briefly to where we started. Look again at Luke 8:15. How can you be a disciple of Christ who perseveres and stands firm in this ever changing world? Ask God to help you be such a woman.

Day 5 – Trusting God's Word Above All Else

Reading on My Front Porch

Read: Psalm 19:7-11 in your Bible. The words "law, testimony, precepts, commandments, and judgments" are all used here as synonyms for the Bible or the Word of God. According to this Psalm of David, how much does he esteem God's Word?

Visiting on My Front Porch

I have to admit that for the early years of my life as a believer I saw the Bible as a wise book with good advice, but not necessarily the answer to every question in life. I assumed it was somewhat outdated and that parts of it were no longer really relevant to our modern lives. While I read my Bible regularly as a teenager and a young adult, I didn't always give it final authority. For instance, during my college years in the early 1980s I began to embrace the ideas of feminism and choice (abortion). I suppose because I was just really forming my ideas of what it means to be a woman, I welcomed most any opinion that sounded good to me. In my early 20s it seemed important to have freedoms, potential in the marketplace, opportunities for advancement, and independence. I also had friends who had chosen homosexual relationships. While the thought of same sex relationships seemed odd to me, I felt like my friends deserved the chance to be who they were. These were my friends, after all. They were good, smart, kind people. How could they be wrong?

Just starting out in adulthood and trying to piece together a world that could make sense to me, I often relegated the words of the Bible to being outdated, misinterpreted, or culturally irrelevant. I remember buying a book called *The Hard Sayings of Jesus* with the hopes that it would explain some of these conflicts between the Bible and the accepted standards of our day. But the book only made matters worse because it drew an even starker line between the teachings of the Bible and our cultural norms. I guess I had hoped for a softening of the line instead.

I grew more and more frustrated with the Bible and with God as I continued to read and study my Bible but also listen to the voices on the talk shows, in the magazines, and of my peers. These various voices weren't jiving and I wanted them to.

The problem I had in my early adult years is one that I'm afraid many Christians are still battling. The dilemma is "How do I live by the Bible, accept it as truth, and make it my standard, and still be enlightened, up-to-date, and progressive?" I found the answer to this question when I stopped fighting a losing battle.

God blessed me with some tremendously wise mentors during my early 20s. They were relevant, successful, intelligent, and even beautiful people – the kind of people I wanted to surround myself with at that time (God knew what He was doing!). Over the course of being in their homes, going to lunch with them, and watching them raise their families, I finally became convinced of what I needed to do before life would begin to really make sense.

I needed to decide on one authority for my life and listen to it exclusively. I was listening to advice from too many sources – well-meaning people, the media, the experts, Hollywood, authors, etc. And yes, I was listening to the still small voice of the Holy Spirit too. But His gentle voice was getting drowned out by the other louder, more authoritative sounding voices that were clamoring for my attention. I remember one of my mentors, a young, godly mother of four, telling me that following God's Word would never lead me down the wrong path. I could trust Him to always speak truth, even if it didn't seem to add up at the time. She challenged me to make God's Word the ultimate authority in my life, to assume that any message from any other source was a lie and a deception if it didn't line up with the Bible 100%. Tough mandate, but I was up for the challenge.

I could continue to make this story long and drawn out, but I'll cut to the happy ending instead. Twenty years later I can tell you with assurance that the Bible calls the shots in my life and I don't regret it at all. While it's not always easy to stand firm on the teachings of the Bible, it is always rewarding. I've allowed the Bible to shape my convictions about abortion, homosexuality, marriage, sex, money, legislation, ecology and everything else. While my convictions may put me on the unpopular side of many debates, I know I'm on the side of truth. Not only that, I've experienced firsthand that when I apply God's Word to my life, even when it is uncomfortable, costly, embarrassing, or difficult, He always causes it to work for good in the end. God is faithful to His Word if I am faithful to His Word. For that matter, God is faithful to His Word even if I am not. His Word is true and trustworthy, but you will never know that completely until you allow it to be the *only* authority in your life.

I'm a student at heart. I love to learn. I love to read. I love to pick peoples' brains for information and wisdom. So if I'm going to make the Bible my only authority in life does that mean I must completely stop listening to other voices or reading other material? Absolutely not. But it does mean I need to be much more selective and I need to read and listen with great discernment. 1 John 4:1 tells me to "test the spirits to see whether they are from God." In other words, I need to check out every message against the infallible Word of God and I also need to check out the spirit in which that message was given.

When I was deciding to make the Bible the ultimate authority in my life, I had to choose to trust God's Word above anything else. I have to trust it above:

- my feelings

- the values and traditions I've grown up with

- "educated" opinions

- my culture

Which of these is most difficult for you to submit to the authority of God's Word? Circle it.

I'd like to give you some scriptures to look up that speak to asserting God's Word over each of the things listed above. These scriptures tell us how or why we are to heed God's Word instead of following our feelings, our traditions, "educated" opinions, or the norms of our culture. Here's your assignment. It's a little open-ended but I trust you'll get something out of it. Simply read the scriptures below and jot down how they speak to the issues. You may have to think on a few of them, but that's good for us, right?

God's Word is more trustworthy than *my feelings*.
Psalm 119:28, 50, 143, 169

_____

_____

_____

God's Word is more trustworthy than *the traditions and values with which I was raised*.
Matthew 5:20-22, 27-28, 31-32, 38-40, 43-44

_____

_____

_____

God's Word is more trustworthy than *"educated" opinions.*
Proverbs 3:5-7, 1 Corinthians 1:18-25

_____

_____

_____

God's Word is more trustworthy than the *norms of my culture.*
Isaiah 40:6-8, 55:8-9; Judges 17:6 (Remember this verse? Remember the results?)

_____

_____

_____

Looking Out From My Front Porch
I've been gut-level honest with you today about my struggles to make God's Word the authority in my life. I still have to make a conscious decision almost daily to filter everything else through the supremacy of the Bible. When I've been offended and my feelings are hurt (emotions) I struggle to apply the Bible's mandate to forgive my offender. Because I was raised to be independent and free-thinking (tradition & values), I have to choose to follow God's instruction to submit to my husband. Since I like to read *Woman's Day* and *Good Housekeeping* magazines (educated opinions), I have to question what I read and sometimes disagree with the "experts" based on the authority of the Bible. And as I watch *Good Morning America* most every morning (culture), I have to work to keep God's perspective on what I see going on in our world. The main way I manage to win this constant battle is by spending time in the Bible *daily*. I read it, meditate on it, study it, and even memorize it. I saturate myself in God's Word. It is my authority and I want to know what it says and understand it. Besides that, the more time I spend in God's Word the more I come to love it and depend on it.

Now it's your turn to be honest. How much do you value God's Word? Is it the final authority in your life? Do you view your world through the lens of the Bible? Do you check out everything by it? Do you make your decisions based completely on its teaching? Do you love it and esteem it? **Check only the** *one or two* **answers below that best describe you**. The list of choices continues on the next page.

- ○ I've read at least some of the Bible.

- ○ I've considered the Bible to be a wise book and somewhat historically correct.

- ○ I listen to the teachings of the Bible but I also listen to other teachers, philosophers, etc.

- ○ I have a difficult time telling who knows what is right, whether it be biblical teachers or politicians or talk show guests or writers.

- ○ I struggle making the Bible relevant to our current culture.

- ○ I'm wondering if the Bible is a little outdated and maybe has some mistakes.

- ○ I'm thinking of making the Bible the authority in my life.

    ○ I've chosen to make the Bible the authority in my life, but I still really struggle with obeying it.

    ○ The Bible is my authority in life and I have to saturate myself with it in order to live by it and see my world through its lens.

    ○ I love my Bible! It is my manual for life and I don't know what I'd do without it. It is more precious than gold to me.

Leaving My Front Porch

Before leaving your front porch today, take another look at your world from here. Are you looking at your world through the two important building blocks we discussed this week? Do you remember what they are? First, are you looking at the world through a healthy fear of God? Do you know the true God and is He the authority in your world? Second, are you looking at the world through the pages of the Bible? Is it your manual for understanding and interacting with your world?

I'd like for you to read one more scripture that will serve as the final nail in the reconstructed foundation of our worldview. In Ecclesiastes 12, Solomon, the probable author of the book, is concluding his reflections on life and what it is all about. He has taken a fairly secular or godless approach to looking at the meaning of life in order to draw in those who are trying to live out their days without God. He is reasoning with the best of the humanists and reeling them in with his cynical and philosophical meanderings. After going on and on about life's endless repetition, its futile pursuits, and its failure to thrill, he throws his hands up in the air and agrees with the secular humanists that basically life is pointless. "Vanity of vanities," he says in 12:8. "All is vanity!" But then we realize with Solomon's closing remarks that he has simply been leading us down this futile path so we would arrive at the point of truth, which is found in the 13th verse of Ecclesiastes 12. Solomon knew where he was going all along – straight to the Author of life Himself. And he wisely takes his fellow philosophers to the one place they will find a trustworthy foundation for a correct worldview. It is the same place we have found one in our studies this week.

Please read Ecclesiastes 12:13 in your Bible. According to Solomon, the wisest man ever to live, what two things are necessary for successfully navigating life on this earth, understanding its meaning, and finding joy in one's days?

Talk with God about building a worldview based on a sound knowledge of Him and a high estimation of His Word. Ask Him to help you make any necessary adjustments.

---

[1] Rick Warren & Charles Colson, Wide Angle: Framing Your Worldview (Purpose Driven Ministries and Prison Fellowship, 2006), 13.

Discussion Questions

1. What do you think it means to fear God?

2. How well do you know God? How have you gotten to know Him better over time? What has been most helpful to you in getting to know Him?

3. Have you ever ascribed a wrong characteristic to God? What and why? How did you correct your estimation of God? Do you ever have to rehearse certain attributes of God in order to combat the lies of the enemy? Does that help? Share with your group.

4. Talk in your group about ways you can "speak of all His wonders." What keeps you from doing that more? Does anybody have any tips for making this easier or more natural? Why is this an important part of getting to know your God?

5. Was there any part of Day 4's lesson that helped you rest in the reliability of God's Word with a little more assurance? What proof of reliability speaks the most to you? Why?

6. If someone in your group is still struggling with finding God's Word to be reliable, what are some ways they can investigate its reliability even further?

7. What amazes you most about the Bible?

8. Do you have a harder time trusting God's Word above your feelings, values & traditions, expert opinions, or cultural norms? Why? What can you do about this?

Week 3 – Taking a Fresh Look

> *Once you accept the idea of a created order, a world with intention and design, a world that comes from a Creator, then certain things come into focus, and you discover that the natural order gives us the key ingredients of the good life.*
>
> Charles Colson[1]

Now that we've agreed on some essentials for framing a Christian worldview (a knowledge and fear of the true God and a high estimation of the Bible's authority) it's time to take a fresh look at our world. This week we'll look at a few of the hot topics in our culture from our properly reconstructed front porches. We'll address some worldviews that starkly contrast a biblical worldview and decide how to respond to them.

Day 1 – Won't We All Get to Heaven?

Reading on My Front Porch

Read: 1 John 4:1-6 in your Bible. According to this passage, how can you know if a spiritual teaching or a worldview is from God or not?

Visiting on My Front Porch

Recently I had a discussion about spiritual things with a friend I'll call Samantha. My friend is not a Christian, but she has researched and studied most every popular religion from Mormonism to Buddhism, from Wicca to New Age philosophy. She will admit that she is more confused than ever from trying to find a religion that fits her and that she hasn't found one yet. Still she is certain that anyone who sincerely follows any of these religions or others will surely end up in heaven. She assures me that God would not "send anyone to hell" and therefore we will all go to heaven when we die, regardless of which path we take. The problem with Samantha's assertion is that, while it may be based on a thorough study of multiple religions, it is most assuredly not based on any knowledge of the one true God.

Unfortunately many people in our postmodern world agree with Samantha. They insist that all roads lead to heaven and the only reason some people are on one road while others are taking a different path is so that we can all have our pick of religions. Why not? We get to pick our ice cream flavor, our baseball team and our hamburger condiments. Why shouldn't we get to choose how we get to God? I'll tell you why: because there's only one road that leads to a relationship with God and that is by way of the cross.

Read the discussion between Jesus and His disciples from John 14:1-6 below. Then answer the questions that follow.

1"Do not let your hearts be troubled. Trust in God; trust also in me. 2 In my Father's house are many rooms; if it were not so, I would have told you. I am going there to prepare a place for you. 3 And if I go and prepare a place for you, I will come back and take you to be with me that you also may be where I am. 4You know the way to the place where I am going."

5 Thomas said to him, "Lord, we don't know where you are going, so how can we know the way?"

6 Jesus answered, "I am the way and the truth and the life. No one comes to the Father except through me. (NIV)

1. Where is Jesus going and why is He going there? _____

    _____

2. Does he want his disciples to join Him there? _____ Does He want them to know how to get there? _____ How do you know? _____

    _____

3. Circle the sentence that tells Jesus' followers how to get to His Father's house.

4. Underline the sentence that indicates whether or not there are multiple paths to take.

One of the characteristics of our culture is that we like choices. We want our vote to count, our voice to be heard, and our opinion to be polled. We demand to be able to choose from a variety of cell phone plans, postage stamp styles, grocery stores, specialty coffees, and salad dressings. We're frustrated when there aren't enough different types of magazines to read at the doctor's office and we choose restaurants based on whether they carry our choice of cola or not. Everything we buy comes in a multitude of colors, flavors, styles, sizes, and prices so we can choose what's best for us. We like to choose.

And when it comes to going to heaven, we *do* get to choose. We choose God or we choose false gods. We choose Jesus or we reject Him. We choose obedience or rebellion. We choose the Bible or false teaching. We choose heaven or hell. I repeat: *we* choose heaven or hell; God never chooses to send anyone to hell. On that one point my friend Samantha is right on the money. Read 2 Peter 3:9.

What does God choose for all of us?_____

_____

And how do we choose heaven? Turn to John 3 in your Bible and read verses 1-21. In this passage Jesus is telling Nicodemus, one of the Pharisees, how to be saved – how to have a right relationship with God and go to heaven.

Match the scripture verses on the left with the corresponding teaching on the right.

1. John 3:3   _____ Those who do not believe in Jesus are judged.

2. John 3:15   _____ You have to be born again to see the kingdom of God.

3. John 3:16   _____ There are many who love the lives they live in the darkness and want nothing to do with Jesus.

4. John 3:17   _____ Those who choose to believe in Jesus have eternal life.

5. John 3:18   _____ Jesus didn't come to judge the world, but to save the world.

6. John 3:19-20   _____ God sent His Son Jesus because He loves all of us.

Friends, we decided last week that God's Word is our final authority. It is true and trustworthy. If that is the case, then we have the one and only way to have a relationship with God and a reservation in His kingdom mapped out clearly for us in John 3. And if Jesus' own directions for salvation in this passage leave any question as to whether there is another way, we know that He said in John 14:6 that He alone is the way to have a relationship with God the Father. That brings us to one last crucial question.

Is Jesus who He says He is? Well, ladies, He either is the only begotten Son of the Father, God Himself, and the "way, the truth, and the life" or He is a fool, a habitual liar, a crazy person, and a dangerous psychopath. There is no room for Him to be a good teacher, a wise master, a spiritual guru, a prophet, or a forerunner of the true Messiah. He never claimed to be any of those things; He only claimed to be God. He either is or He isn't.

Looking Out From My Front Porch

According to the scholastically sound information provided by Wikipedia (don't you just love it!), *"religious pluralism* is a term used to describe the acceptance of all religious paths as equally valid, promoting coexistence." Read that definition one more time and underline or highlight it. Religious pluralism is part of a widely accepted worldview that denies that there is one true way to God. This is not a biblical worldview, but it is one that many Christians have bought into because the wise and educated of this world espouse such a view and promote it incessantly – in the school systems, in the work place, in the media, and in the court system. Unfortunately, while pluralists demand that all other religions be given respect and understanding, they seldom give the same respect to true Christianity. For instance, in many school systems in America teachers are provided state approved curriculum for teaching children about the celebrations of Kwanza, Ramadan and Hanukkah (including spiritual significance), but they are not allowed to even mention the spiritual roots of Christmas. No Christmas carols, no nativity scenes, no mention of Jesus. While most courts have found such treatment to be unconstitutional, this kind of "exclusive pluralism" continues to go on all over our country.

According to what we've learned today, what do you think the Christian response should be to religious pluralism? How should you respond when confronted with it head-on, for instance, in your child's school?

_____

_____

_____

Leaving My Front Porch

My bet is you have friends, family or neighbors like my friend Samantha. They're looking for a way to God, a road to heaven, and yet they're headed down one of many wrong paths. And if you try to tell them about Jesus, the way, the truth and the life, they become offended that you are pushing your brand of religion on them.

You feel like you've been banging your head against a brick wall in an effort to persuade them that Jesus is the way. You may feel defeated and agitated that there seems no way to reach them. I understand; I've felt that way too. But let's not grow weary in praying for our lost friends and family. Remember, God so loved my friend Samantha that He sent His only begotten Son to die for her. He's not given up on her and I won't either.

Before you leave your front porch today, look out from it and consider those who are still searching for God. Pray for God to draw them to Him. Pray for softened hearts and open doors. And make yourself a willing instrument through which God can show them the one true way.

Day 2 – Why the Beginning Matters

Reading on My Front Porch

Read: Genesis chapters 1 & 2 in your Bible. I know this is a lot of reading. Today you'll be reading more of the Bible and less of me. Enjoy these two familiar chapters afresh and with enthusiasm.

Visiting on My Front Porch

It's oh so crucial for us to be clear on how our world came into existence. That foundation will help you answer so many of life's questions:

- Are we accountable to anyone or free to do as we choose?
- Do I have a purpose?
- Are some things more important in this world than others? What's priority?
- What is the relationship between mankind and the earth? Should we worship it? Should we assume that things in nature have a spirit? Or should we really care at all about nature?
- Is life on this earth as fragile as some say? Could it all be destroyed tomorrow by hairspray and carbon monoxide?
- Do I really have any responsibility toward the earth?
- Could we have evolved from tadpoles or monkeys? Will we continue to evolve or have we arrived at a state of superiority?
- Are some races inferior to others? Should we help evolution out by simply annihilating those who are inferior?
- Is work a curse that should be avoided at all cost?

Did you recognize some of the questions above as being the basis for some current and past worldviews? I bet you did. The question of the world's beginning is crucial to how we treat each other, the natural world around us, and our God.

Okay. I promised you that you would read less from me today. I'm going to make good on that promise! You'll need your Bible to answer the questions below.

Based on your reading in Genesis 1-2, answer the following multiple choice questions.

1. Who created the world (1:1)?

   ___ our spirits   ___ no one   ___ a big bang   ___ God

2. How did God create the world (1:3, 6, 9, etc.)?

   ___ God spoke it   ___ God threw fire balls   ___ God used what was already here

3. How many days did God take to create the world and all that is in it (1:31-2:3)?

   ___ 1   ___ 7   ___ 6   ___ 2,439,975,666

4. What interesting thing did God do after He created the creatures of the sea, air, and land (1:22, 28)?

   ___ He cried   ___ He redid them   ___ He blessed them   ___ He quit

5. What was unique about God's creation of man (1:26-27)?

    ___ Man was created from the monkey.

    ___ Man was created first.

    ___ Man was created in God's image.

    ___ Man was created as an amoeba and evolved into a man much later.

    (Can you tell I'm having some fun with this? ☺)

6. What did God instruct the people to do after creating them (1:28)? (More than one)

    ___ be fruitful   ___ multiply   ___ subdue the earth   ___ rule over animals

7. What was God's final estimation of all He had created (1:31)?

    ___ it would do   ___ He didn't like it   ___ it was very good   ___ so what?

8. How did God supply water for the plants and animals in the beginning (2:5-6)?

    ___ it rained 40 days   ___ there was no need   ___ a mist rose from the earth

9. What is man's origin (2:7)?

    ___ fish   ___ apes   ___ dust (dirt)   ___ we don't know

10. How did man become a living being (2:7)?

    ___ magic   ___ God breathed into him the breath of life   ___ a big bang

11. Where did God put the man (2:8)?

    ___ in the ocean   ___ in a garden He planted   ___ no where   ___ in Egypt

12. Why did God put him there (2:15)?

    ___ to relax and drink tropical punch   ___ to cultivate and keep it   ___ to suffer

13. Why did God create the woman, Eve (2:18)? (more than one)

    ___ He didn't want Adam to be alone

    ___ He hadn't done so well on Adam and wanted to do better

    ___ Adam couldn't find his way around and wouldn't ask for directions

    ___ He wanted Adam to have a suitable helper

14. How did the animals get their names (2:19)?

    ___ they came with labels   ___ they named themselves   ___ Adam named them

15. How did God create the woman (2:21-22)?

    ___ the same way He made Adam

    ___ He fashioned her beginning with one of Adam's ribs

    ___ He spoke her into existence

16. What was the man supposed to do with the woman (2:24)?

    ___ mock her   ___ leave her   ___ cleave to her   ___ ignore her

Good job! Now look back at the questions about life that I gave in bulleted form at the beginning of this portion of the lesson. After carefully examining the Bible's account of creation from Genesis 1 & 2, do you feel like you have some answers to any of those questions? Using the information from Genesis 1 & 2 try to give at least an initial answer to at least three of those questions; you can choose which ones you answer.

_____

_____

_____

_____

_____

_____

I'm not implying that you can completely and exhaustively answer these life questions by just studying Genesis 1 & 2. You would need to apply other scriptures as well if you wanted to fully answer these questions. But can you see how a good foundational knowledge of how the earth was created would be the first step in resolving most of these issues? For instance, if someone doesn't believe God created the earth then that person also will not believe they are accountable to God. Why should they be? And if a person doesn't understand the order and the intricacies of the creation process and doesn't know that man was told to cultivate the earth and subdue the animals, they might assume that we are all on equal footing with the animals. They might even believe that animals are our "brothers and sisters" with whom we *share* this planet on level ground. Finally, and quite conversely, if a person doesn't know that man was told to cultivate the earth and tend to the animals they might assume they have absolutely no responsibility in taking care of the earth. Does any of this sound like some of the views you have heard expressed in our culture recently?

Looking Out From My Front Porch
Many of the current worldviews begin with the assumption that the earth and life simply evolved. The proponents of these worldviews, such as *naturalism* and *humanism*, have taken God out of the mix, largely because if He did create the earth then He is also in charge of it.

Why would a naturalist or humanist remove God from their explanation of the world's origin? In other words, how would the absence or disassociation of God benefit someone?

_____

_____

_____

Many people remove God from their explanation of how the world began simply because they don't want Him to be in charge of it. They don't want the earth, the people of the earth, and the souls of people to belong to Him. They also know that if a superior, holy, righteous, and just God created them, then they would be accountable to Him. They don't want to be accountable to Him. They want to call their own shots, do it their way, and claim full possession of everything they have and do. Finally, even if they acknowledge a Creator, many people, such as *deists*, believe He is uninvolved at this point – that He simply set the world in motion and stepped back to view from a point of little interest. This way "intelligent, gifted, wise people" can determine where we are going and they can share their knowledge with the rest of us from a place of superiority. They may even ignite a little fear in us. On the surface such lines of thought may seem enlightened and freeing, but don't be fooled. If you look closely you'll find that each of these philosophies, and others, are fueled primarily by pride – the armor worn by every enemy of God.

Read James 4:6 in your Bible. What are God's reactions to the proud and to the humble?

To the proud - _____

To the humble - _____

Dear friend, if the Bible is your authority you must hold onto all of it with a firm grasp. Even if the creation account seems impossibly crazy to you, believe it with all of your heart. Let's face it; the big bang theory is much crazier anyhow. And when you are confronted with mysteries surrounding the creation story that you cannot explain or comprehend, bend the knee in humble confession that He is God and you are not. God will honor such humility with the grace you need to strengthen and stretch your faith. But He will go to war against the prideful woman who insists on having answers before she will submit to a Creator God.

When you have nailed down your faith that God created the world just as He says He did, you will be able to navigate safely through the worldviews that are contrary to the Bible and you will be able to please your God.

Leaving My Front Porch

Before we leave our porches today let's read one final scripture. This will be our benediction as we turn these verses into our prayer. Read Hebrews 11:1-3 & 6. Then ask God to build your faith.

Day 3 – What's This Life All About?

Reading on My Front Porch

Read: Colossians 1:16 in your Bible. Consider this verse in light of yesterday's lesson on creation. According to Colossians 1:16, why were you and I created?

Visiting on My Front Porch

Not only will a foundational understanding of God's creation of this world make a difference in how you view the world, but a similar understanding of how and why God created *you* will affect what you expect from this life. And what you expect from life will strongly impact how you view the world. Do you see the world as a playground or a mission field? Do you see the people of this world as your servants, your fellow pilgrims, your enemies, or God's creation? Do you see the events of this world as random, spiraling out of control, mysterious, or permitted by a God of grace? Do you see your personal experiences as inconveniences, unfair punishments, random situations, cosmic coincidences, or part of God's development program designed specifically for you? And just what do you think the ultimate goal is in this life? Are we all trying to die richer than our parents, build a comfortable nest, experience as much adventure as possible, leave our mark on the world, prove ourselves, or…what?

Read Romans 11:36 below. Circle the word that indicates what we owe God.

For from Him and through Him and to Him are all things. To Him be the glory forever!

Amen. (NIV)

According to this scripture, all things, including our lives, are gifts *from* God, powered and supplied *through* God, and accountable and ultimately returned *to* God. Because He is the initiator of our lives, the power behind them, and the goal at the end of them, we owe Him glory every day. But exactly what does that mean? What does it mean to give God glory or to glorify Him?

According to the *Vine's Complete Expository Dictionary of Old and New Testament Words*, the Greek word translated glory is *doxa*. It signifies an opinion, an estimate, reputation, or accurate reflection of something. *Doxazo*, the Greek verb translated glorify, is similar in definition. It means to ascribe to, acknowledge as, and magnify or bring into full view. With those definitions in hand let's see if we can get a little better handle on what it really means to give God glory or to glorify Him. I don't know about you, but I heard those two terms on a weekly basis in church for more years than I care to count before I ever heard them adequately defined. If you and I are going to fulfill the Romans 11:36 mandate to give God glory forever and ever we had better know what that means!

Look again at the definitions for glory and glorify that I provided in the preceding paragraph. Highlight or underline them so they are further etched in your mind. Drawing upon those two definitions and putting aside any preconceived ideas about the words, write in the blanks below what you think it means to glorify God or give glory to God.

_____

_____

When I give God glory I acknowledge who He truly is. Through my actions, words, and demeanor I put a magnifying spotlight on Him and provide the people around me with an accurate picture of who He is. I reflect His character, His ways, and His Word so that others see a correct estimate of the one true God. Let me break this down a little further. When I allow my emotions and reasoning to lead me, people get a very revealing picture of who Kay Harms is, but when I obey God's Word and walk by His Spirit I give the world an accurate view of my God. If I forgive one who has offended me, I shine a magnifying light on God's grace and mercy. If I remain patient and gentle with my children, people get a glimpse of my kind and patient Father in Heaven. And if I give generously to others without reproach, I show the world that I have a God who lavishes His blessings on me without hesitation and provides my every need. I can't glorify God in this way unless I have the power of Jesus working in me. I can't do it on my own.

So often we think of glorifying God through verbal praises and songs of worship. While we certainly can and should give God glory through worshipful songs, lifted hands, and bowed heads, I believe we're missing the greater opportunity for glorifying God if we fail to recognize the need to give Him glory through obedient lives, day in and day out. Quite simply, we glorify God when we act like His children, His offspring. Just as my children look somewhat like me, walk similarly to me, and even speak like me, my actions, words, and countenance should be a striking resemblance to my Father. Then those around me who have yet to meet Him will get an accurate picture of what He is like and they'll desire to be introduced. That is what it means to give God a little glory. And that, sweet friend, is our purpose.

Now that we understand a little better the *purpose* of our lives, let's see if we can also gain a better grasp on the *meaning* of life. How does it work? Why is it so hard? Where is it leading and does it really matter how I navigate it?

In his book *The Purpose Driven Life*, Rick Warren explores much more thoroughly than I can this question of "Why am I here?" If you haven't read this thought provoking book, I encourage you to do so. Warren's book helps clearly define this element of a biblical worldview. But for today's lesson I'd like to gently lift a very important outline from his book, giving him all the credit for coming up with this wise approach to nailing down the meaning of life.

Warren suggests that most of us have at some time used one or more metaphors to describe life. Have you ever said, "Life is like a rollercoaster!" or "Life is like a carousel: sometimes you're up and sometimes you're down!" Comedic writer Erma Bombeck played on one such metaphor with the title she gave one of her most popular books, *If Life is a Bowl of Cherries, What Am I Doing In the Pits?* I think she has something there! Others, even Christian teachers and authors, have likened life to a puzzle, a symphony, a dance, a race or a journey. But Warren provides three fresh metaphors for life that I think are scriptural and helpful in building a biblical worldview that approaches this question from God's perspective. According to Warren, life is a:

- **Test** – "God continually tests people's character, faith, obedience, love, integrity, and loyalty. Words like *trials*, *temptations*, *refining*, and *testing* occur more than 200 times in the Bible…Character is both developed and revealed by tests, and all of life is a test."[2]

- **Trust** – "Our time on earth and our energy, intelligence, opportunities, relationships, and resources are all gifts from God that he has entrusted to our care and management. We are stewards of whatever God gives us…At the end of your life on earth you will be evaluated and rewarded according to how well you handled what God entrusted to you. That means *everything* you do, even simple daily chores, has eternal implications."[3]

- **Temporary Assignment** – "To make the best use of your life, you must never forget two truths: First, compared with eternity, life is extremely brief. Second, earth is only a temporary residence. You won't be here long, so don't get too attached…In order to keep us from becoming too attached to earth, God allows us to feel a significant amount of discontent and dissatisfaction in life – longings that will *never* be fulfilled on this side of eternity."[4]

Just so we can see that Warren's approach is biblical I'd like for us to look at some supporting scriptures for each metaphor. *Please read the following passages in your Bible and match them with the appropriate metaphor on the right.* As you read the passages also take note of *what pleases God*. In light of these three metaphors, what kind of person pleases God along the way? Jot down any notes in the blanks below.

_____ Genesis 1:28-30	A.	Life is a test.
_____ Genesis 22:1-13	B.	Life is a trust.
_____ Deuteronomy 8:16	C.	Life is a temporary assignment.
_____ Joshua 14:14		
_____ Job 2:3-10		
_____ Psalm 26:2		
_____ Psalm 84:5		
_____ Isaiah 43:18-19		
_____ Daniel 12:13		
_____ Matthew 6:19-20		
_____ Matthew 25:14-30		
_____ 1 Corinthians 4:1-2		
_____ 2 Corinthians 4:18		
_____ Philippians 3:20		
_____ Hebrews 11:13-16		
_____ James 1:2-4		
_____ James 4: 13-14		

_____

_____

_____

_____

Looking Out From My Front Porch

One of the most prominent worldviews that comes out of a misconception about life's meaning is "materialism." Yes, materialism is a worldview. Here's the definition straight from another wonderful Internet source of wisdom and knowledge, www.answers.com:

Materialism:

1. The theory or attitude that physical well-being and worldly possessions constitute the greatest good and highest value in life.
2. A great or excessive regard for worldly concerns.

3. Generally: belief that all that matters is material welfare, as opposed to spiritual or other ideals.[5]

For the materialist, *life is a shopping spree.*

Another prominent worldview that stands in stark contrast to Warren's three Ts is "hedonism." Here's a definition for this popular worldview:

Hedonism is the philosophy that pleasure is of ultimate importance, the most important pursuit. The name derives from the Greek word for "delight".[6]

Hedonists basically only do what is fun, pleasurable, or easy for themselves. For a hedonist, *life is a party.*

A third worldview that we need to be aware of is "egoism." **Egoism** is the belief that an individual should only be motivated by self-interest and ought to only do what is in their best self-interest. It denies that anyone ought to be accountable to anyone else. To an egoist, *life is a lingering look in the mirror.*

Now, with all that information in hand, match the unbiblical worldview with the appropriate "T" that it *directly contrasts.*

Materialism	Life is a Test
Hedonism	Life is a Trust
Egoism	Life is a Temporary assignment

In my estimation, materialism directly denies that life is a temporary assignment (forget the mansion in heaven, I'll build one now!), hedonism resists the notion that life is a test (that's no fun!), and egoism disclaims the accountability required if life is a trust (you're not the boss of me!). You may have answered differently; that's okay. I just wanted you to have to think it through.

Leaving My Front Porch

Most of us suffer a little bit from one or more of these unbiblical worldviews if we're honest. We've all looked at situations and made decisions based purely on "how it affects me" (egoism). Many of us are guilty of accumulating too much stuff (materialism). And I'm sure most of us have shirked away from some act of service because it just didn't look like much fun (hedonism). Let's close today by asking God to show us if we're looking at life wrong. Confess that you agree with Him that life is indeed a test, a trust, and a temporary assignment. Ask for help living in light of those truths.

Day 4 – Old Fashioned or Glorious?

Reading on My Front Porch

Read: Genesis 2:18-25 & 4:1 in your Bible. From reading these passages, what do you think God's plan for sex is? Be as specific as possible. (Specific, not elicit! ☺)

Visiting on My Front Porch

Sex is definitely one of the hot topics in our culture. Most every magazine you see in the rack at the grocery store will have at least one teaser about a sex article on its cover. And most of the time the teaser indicates that the article promotes views about sex that are quite contrary to God's standard presented in the Bible. Once again, due to being saturated in the world's view of sex, many Christians have lost the biblical view. Today we're going to try to nail down some biblical precepts about sex so we can wisely discern the wrong messages being sent to us through television shows, movies, novels, magazines, and advertisers. We need to know the truth about sex, God's plan and standards for it, so we can practice healthy and holy (yes holy) sexuality ourselves, and so we can pass down the right viewpoint to our children and others.

First, I think we can establish from the scriptures we read in Genesis 2 and 4 that God created sex to be a natural and beneficial part of the marriage relationship between one woman and one man. That's the parameters He set for sex, but that is also the confines in which it is best and most freely enjoyed, regardless of what we may have been led to believe by our permissive and unrestrained culture. For more biblical references to back up this precept you can read Ruth 4:13; 1 Samuel 1:19; Song of Solomon 6:11-8:14; 1 Corinthians 7:3-5; Ephesians 5:25-33; 1 Timothy 3:2 and Hebrews 13:4. We'll look at scriptures that give God's opinion of other types of sex shortly. First let's read Elizabeth Elliot's words about the gift and confines of sex:

> *Like every other good gift that comes down from the Father of Lights, the gift of sexual activity is meant to be used as He intended, within the clearly defined limits of His purpose, which is marriage. If marriage is not included in God's will for an individual, then sexual activity is not included either…To offer my body to the Lord as a living sacrifice includes offering to Him my sexuality and all that that entails, even my unfulfilled longings.*[7]

Elizabeth's view stands in stark contrast to the views on just about every television program you can watch today. Deny yourself just because you haven't found the person to marry? In a culture where it's popular to order dessert before the main course, whip out the credit card for things we can't afford, and pay $5.00 for a cup of coffee, that idea is considered completely outlandish. But God never changed the purpose and confines of sex, even though people throughout the ages have certainly pushed the envelope on this issue. Yes, some of God's right-hand men even took more than one wife and had concubines (mistresses) to boot, but that doesn't mean God told them that was right or blessed those relationships. If you know anything about David's family life, you know that his multiple marriages produced envy, rivalry, and even murder among his children. God's blessing was obviously not on those relationships and David paid the price for his sin.

One of the most significant ways our culture has soft-pedaled around sexual sins is to rename them with much less offensive and sometimes even glamorous titles. Today we're going to name these sexual sins what God names them so we can begin to rebuild a biblical worldview in the area of sex. We're going to do this in a way that allows you to search the Bible yourself to find out what God says about sexual activity while also exposing and debunking the "prettier" titles the world has given to sexual sins.

Read the scriptures in the left-hand column. Write a 3-6 word summary of each. Match the principle found there with the world's name for that sexual activity in the column on the right. Then, in the space provided, write the biblical or accurate name for it.

Leviticus 20:10 & Matthew 5:27-28   "sleeping together"_____

Hebrews 13:4   "having an affair" _____

Romans 1:22-27 & 1 Cor. 6:9-10   "celibate marriage"_____

James 1:14-16   "lesbian or gay"   _____

1 Corinthians 7:3-5   "adult entertainment" _____
                                           (The more accurate word isn't named in
                                           scripture, but you know what it is.)

When we use the more accurate and biblical terms for sexual sins, we learn to deal with them as sins and not just personal preferences. The Bible calls any type of sexual immorality *fornication*. It's an ugly word, as it ought to be. Sin is ugly, not pretty or glamorous or sophisticated. In the narrower sense, the word *fornication* is used to describe pre-marital sex or sex between two people, neither of whom are married. Hollywood simply calls that sleeping together, as though it is perfectly innocent.

Adultery is voluntary sexual intercourse between a married person and a person who is not his or her spouse. Jesus raised the bar on sexual purity when He said that even if one lusts in his heart after someone who is not his spouse he has committed adultery (Matthew 5:27-28). God hates adultery. In the Old Testament the penalty for adultery was death. Today we don't even come close to stoning those who commit adultery, but they potentially suffer all sorts of deaths nonetheless. Adultery can kill integrity, marriages, families, careers, and even one's health.

Sex before and outside of marriage has become common, anticipated, and even expected. Sexual purity seems like an outdated ideal with no benefits. But in fact God created sex and He knows that any sexual activity outside those parameters is dangerous and self-defeating.

In what ways might it be destructive to have sex outside of the confines of marriage?

_____

_____

_____

The word *homosexual* refers to sexual acts, sexual inclinations, or affinities toward a person of the same gender. The words *gay* and *lesbian* are cultural attempts to remove the stigma of homosexuality. In 1 Corinthians 6:9-10, homosexuality is prohibited by God. It is not part of God's plan for the people He created and it is not His plan for sex. Regardless of how many votes we may take, how many court rulings there may be, and how many homosexuals may be depicted in primetime sitcoms, homosexuality is not okay in God's eyes. In fact, in Leviticus 18:22 God calls homosexuality "an abomination" and in Leviticus 20:13 He says it is "detestable." Do you see any wiggle room there? Romans 1:22-27 provides us with a better understanding of the degenerate thinking that can lead to this sin. People are not born homosexual, regardless of how that may appear to be the case. However, people are born with a sin nature and certain experiences, thought patterns, unfulfilled emotional needs and choices can lead a person toward that sin. The passage in Romans makes that very clear.

One of the less talked about sexual sins is the sin of *withholding sex* from one's spouse. Remember in Genesis how God said that a man and woman would cleave to one another in marriage and become "one flesh"? When you enter into marriage you *give* your body to your spouse; it is no longer your own. We read in 1 Corinthians 7:3-5 that the only reason to deprive one's spouse of sexual satisfaction is for a mutually agreed upon and temporary "time out" for the purpose of prayer or seeking God. Truthfully, few of us can claim that as an excuse for refusing our partner sex! Because the marriage relationship should be a loving and sacrificial one, this does not give license for abuse. There may be other valid reasons for a couple not to have sex, but they should be infrequent if at all possible. The bottom line is that sex or the lack thereof should not become a manipulation tactic in a marriage.

What do you think in fact are the more common reasons one spouse would *withhold sex* from the other? Are these valid reasons according to scripture?

_____

_____

_____

Finally we need to get real about one final sexual sin that has become disturbingly prevalent in our culture: *pornography*. James 1:14-16 reminds us that sin begins when "lust has conceived." Realizing that you are tempted is not a sin, but when you let that temptation fester in your mind and you invite in a few thoughts or images to entertain that temptation, you have begun to sin. Lest you think this is a sexual sin that only besets men, approximately 17% of women struggle with an addiction to pornography. Today pornographic images are not just available in "girlie magazines", but on regular television, on the Internet, and in movies. Quite honestly, all of us need to do a "pornography check". We need to evaluate how many times on a regular basis our eyes view images that are harmful to our sexual purity. And we need to make a thorough plan for putting an end to such viewing. We need to adopt some standards and they will surely cause us to appear old-fashioned and nerdy in comparison to our peers, but that is the price of a biblical worldview in the area of sex.

Looking Out From My Front Porch
The 60s and 70s ushered in the age of sexual freedom. Women burned their bras, swingers switched partners by throwing their house keys into a lottery, and couples moved in together without getting married. At the time, such acts seemed outlandish and bold. Today they seem tame and acceptable. Now homosexuals are out of their closets,

pornography is available without leaving your home, and couples have children together without ever planning to marry. Are we just stuck in a world where sex has no parameters or is there anything we can do to stop the mayhem? What do you think?

Leaving My Front Porch

I can't even begin to know what might be the biggest issue that battles for your sexual purity. I do know that whatever tempts you to forfeit that purity is probably a strong and persuasive voice. It seems that's how it is with sexual temptations. Satan found something he can lure most every man and woman into when he happened upon sexual perversion. But let's remember that sex itself was not created by Satan. It is a gift from God meant to be enjoyed within the parameters of marriage. In that safe environment it brings unity, deepened love, pleasure, and intimacy. Outside those parameters, it brings frustration, guilt, shame, regret, disease, judgment, and even death.

Pray today that God will help you be a strong voice in a culture sinking in the depths of sexual depravity. I don't mean to sound overly alarming, but God will not bless a marriage, a family, a church, a community, or a nation that doesn't even bat an eye at the evils of sexual sins. We all need to be a little more chaste. Ask God to give you a renewed fervor for sexual purity.

Day 5 – One Nation Under God

Reading on My Front Porch

Read: Deuteronomy 8:1-20 in your Bible. This passage contains God's words spoken specifically to the nation of Israel just before they took possession of the Promised Land. We shouldn't apply *specific* promises and commands that God gave to Israel to the United States; however, we can apply broad principles. We see from this passage much of how God deals with nations. Summarize what you learn about the kind of nation God blesses.

Visiting on My Front Porch

The Bible is full of examples of how God responded to nations who submitted to His authority and honored Him and how He treated those that disobeyed His commands and worshipped other gods. While the Bible does not contain the full accounts of God's dealings with all nations, we do have several indicators that He is patient, gracious and fair with all nations, but that He ultimately deals justice to those who rebel against Him, treat His chosen people badly, or stubbornly worship other gods.

Read the following scriptures and note what they say about how God relates to the nations.

Deuteronomy 9: 1-5 _____

_____

Deuteronomy 12: 29-31 _____

_____

Deuteronomy 30:17-18 _____

_____

Deuteronomy 30:19-20 _____

_____

2 Chronicles 7:13-14 _____

_____

Job 12:23 _____

_____

Psalm 22:28 _____

_____

Jonah 1:1-2; 3:1-10; 4:11 (Nineveh was the capital of Assyria, a pagan country.)_____

_____

Revelation 7:9 _____

_____

Do you think God has blessed America? _____yes   _____ no

If so, then how has God blessed America? _____

_____

Do you notice any indications that God may have removed His hand of blessing from our

country, as He said He would do if a nation dishonored Him? Explain. _____

_____

According to the scriptures you read, what do we need to do in order for God to continue

to bless America?_____

Looking Out From My Front Porch

The United States of America was founded and established upon a devotion to the true God and obedience to His Word. The people who first settled this country were escaping religious persecution and a state-controlled church that kept them from worshipping God the way they wanted to. They prayed for guidance and safety as they journeyed to this land and ventured onto its undeveloped shores. They depended on God's favor and blessing as they set up the original settlements and tried to farm in a new continent. And they pleaded for God's protection and provision as they experienced cold winters, ravaging illnesses, and confrontations with the natives of the new land. Because they had found this land by God's grace, survived the initial years at His mercy, and begun to reap the bounty of God's blessing, they remembered Him when they began to establish their government. Our government was founded upon a dependence on God, an acknowledgement of His sovereignty, and an allegiance to His Word.

Read the following quotes from some of our country's founding fathers. Highlight or underline any phrases that indicate a distinctly Christian worldview.

"The general principles upon which the Fathers achieved independence were the general principals of Christianity… I will avow that I believed and now believe that those general principles of Christianity are as eternal and immutable as the existence and attributes of God." *John Adams, in a letter written to Abigail on the day the Declaration of Independence was approved by Congress*

"Why is it that, next to the birthday of the Savior of the world, your most joyous and most venerated festival returns on this day [the Fourth of July]? Is it not that, in the chain of human events, the birthday of the nation is indissolubly linked with the birthday of the Savior? That it forms a leading event in the progress of the Gospel dispensation? Is it not that the Declaration of Independence first organized the social compact on the foundation of the Redeemer's mission upon earth? That it laid the cornerstone of human government upon the first precepts of Christianity"? *John Quincy Adams, 1837, at the age of 69, when he delivered a Fourth of July speech at Newburyport, Massachusetts*

"God governs in the affairs of man. And if a sparrow cannot fall to the ground without his notice, is it probable that an empire can rise without His aid? We have been assured in the Sacred Writings that except the Lord build the house, they labor in vain that build it. I firmly believe this. I also believe that, without His concurring aid, we shall succeed in this political building no better than the builders of Babel." *Benjamin Franklin, Constitutional Convention of 1787*

"It cannot be emphasized too clearly and too often that this nation was founded, not by religionists, but by Christians; not on religion, but on the gospel of Jesus Christ. For this very reason, peoples of other faiths have been afforded asylum, prosperity, and freedom of worship here." *Patrick Henry, May 1765 Speech to the House of Burgesses*

Lest we question whether Christians have the right or obligation to attempt to keep this country "under God," we need to keep in mind that our founding fathers would *expect* that of us. Otherwise they have labored in vain. I imagine we have no idea the price many of them paid to establish this country as a Christian nation. We should not be surprised when we have to pay a price as well.

Those of us who have always lived in this country or other democratic nations tend to take the "climate" we enjoy for granted. No, I'm not talking about the weather. By climate I'm referring to basically three things that Americans hold dear and that set us apart from many other nations: hope, freedom, and happiness. When you consider the poverty, political unrest, personal constraints, and religious oppression that exists in so many countries you realize that indeed our founding fathers put together something that has really worked. More accurately, you realize that God has indeed blessed the foundation upon which they built our country. Only in a Christian society can people, even those who are not believers but simply live among those who are, enjoy all three of those blessings with security. Indeed it is in Christ that we find hope (Colossians 1:27), freedom (Galatians 5:1), and happiness (Psalm 1:1-2). If we want America to continue to be a nation that provides hope, freedom, and happiness for those who call it home, we will need to do everything in our power to keep our nation under our God's hand of blessing.

The worldview that causes us to hesitate in fulfilling this mission is none other than *political correctness*. Akin to tolerance, this view demands that we keep religion, more specifically Christianity, and government separate. It is based not on a government document such as the Constitution or Declaration of Independence, but on a personal letter written by Thomas Jefferson. Even then Jefferson's letter has been greatly misconstrued because he was not asking for the church to stay out of politics, but for the government to keep its hands off the church. Quite a contrast to what many in our country hold to be a "separation of church and state."

Leaving My Front Porch

Thank God for allowing you the opportunity to live in a country that offers its citizens hope, freedom, and happiness. Commit to do your part to continue the legacy of our founding fathers by sharing the gospel one person at a time and letting your light shine.

---

[1] Charles Colson, *The Good Life* (Carol Stream, IL: Tyndale House Publishers, Inc., 2005), 278.

[2] Rick Warren, *The Purpose Driven Life* (Grand Rapids, MI: Zondervan, 2002), 42-43.

[3] Ibid, 44-45.

[4] Ibid, 47-50.

[5] http://www.answers.com/topic/hedonism-theory

[6] http://en.wikipedia.org/wiki/Hedonism

[7] Elizabeth Elliot, *Discipline: The Glad Surrender*, (Old Tappan, NJ: Fleming H. Revell Co., 1982), p. 54.

Discussion Questions

1. What would you tell a friend or co-worker who asked if you thought there was more than one way to get to heaven?

2. What's one new thing you learned from studying the creation account in Genesis? Do you think it's important to believe the creation story to be true and factual? Why or why not?

3. Do you remember the three metaphors for life suggested by Rick Warren? Explain each of those and how you see them played out in your life.

4. Which of the unbiblical worldviews discussed on Day 3 is more of a stumbling block for you: materialism, hedonism, or egoism? Why and how? How do you see these played out in the television shows you watch (or don't watch)?

5. Why is it important for us to name sexual sins accurately? Why do you think our culture shies away from calling these sexual acts what they really are? How hard will it be for you to begin consistently using the biblical names for these sexual sins?

6. What are some of the ways you think God has blessed America? Why has He blessed our country?

7. Do you think any recent events in our country indicate that God is removing His hand of blessing? Does that mean God is bringing judgment on us? Is that fair to the "innocent" people who have suffered? What should we do about this?

Week 4 – The Feminine View

Is...femininity a lost value today? I don't believe it. The world has changed, and most of us live in simple skirts or business suits or jeans instead of flowing gowns. But I still believe that somewhere in the heart of most of us is a little girl who longs to be a lady...I also believe that today's world is hungering to be transformed by the spirit of femininity. What better antidote for an impersonal and violent society than warm, gentle, feminine strength? What better cure for urban sprawl and trashed-out countryside than a love of beauty and confidence in one's ability to make things lovely? What better hope for the future than a nurturing mother's heart that is more concerned for the next generation than for its own selfish desires?

Emilie Barnes[1]

For our final week of study we will look at things from a uniquely feminine perspective. We'll discover God's priority and purposes for women as we study the biblical pattern for womanhood. We'll decide whether feminism is our friend or foe. And we'll see what we as women offer to our world that is unique and needed. Because women contend with two specific and current hot topics more intimately than men do, we'll also take a biblical look at the abortion issue and the definition of beauty.

Day 1 – Are Women Really So Different?

Reading on My Front Porch

Read: Genesis 1:27 & 2:21-22 in your Bible. What word does your translation of Genesis 2:22 use to describe how woman was created?

Visiting on My Front Porch

By this point in the study you have read the complete creation account in Genesis 1 and 2 at least once. Think back or look back in your Bible if you need to. What is the last thing God created?

- ○   the stars
- ○   the man
- ○   ostriches
- ○   the woman
- ○   the flowers

You probably didn't have to think very hard to remember that God's final addition to His world was woman. I don't know about you, but that kind of takes my breath away. I'd never really thought on that detail much before, but it seems pretty special to me that woman was God's last act in the creation drama. In fact, the way the account reads, woman was a sort of encore performance. While we might be inclined to even say He saved the best for last, we'll resist that temptation and just let it suffice that He certainly did save His most interesting method for creating woman. Do you remember how God created everything else? Let's review…

1. God created the heavens, the earth, the plants and the animals by _____ them into existence. (see Genesis 1:3, 6, 9, for instance)

2. God formed man from the _____ of the earth and _____ into him the breath of life.(see Genesis 2:7)

3. God fashioned woman from a _____ taken from the man. (see Genesis 2:22)

Did you know that the word *fashioned* or *built* used in Genesis 2:22 to describe how God created woman is used uniquely to describe this particular part of creation? Genesis 2:22 is the first use of this particular verb. Women are *built*. (And all the men said, "Amen!") While I could creatively, but quite irresponsibly, read all sorts of things into that, I'll resist. I just want us to understand that God designed us women uniquely. He put a little extra effort, creativity, mystery, and elbow grease into the creation of the female. While I don't pretend to know for sure why He did this, I do believe it's significant and worth taking a look at. I think perhaps we were created differently, using a distinctive method, so that we could never doubt that men and women were created to *be* different – to fulfill different roles, to have different needs, to see things differently, to have different dispositions, and to bring something different to the table.

I bring this up on our first day of studying biblical womanhood because I believe we now live in a culture that has tried for some time to minimize the differences between men and women. Oh sure, we highlight those differences when we want to complain that our husband doesn't see something the way we do or when we want to claim such womanly prerogatives as the right to change our minds and the need to own too many shoes, but overall our society has tried to blur the lines between men and women in many ways. Instead of me naming them, why don't you list some of the ways you see less of a distinction between men and women in our culture than in your great-grandmother's day? (They're not all necessarily big or wrong, mind you. I just want us to see how we've minimized the differences that used to be so stark.) I'll get us started.

*men and women now dress similarly*_____   _____

_____   _____

_____   _____

_____   _____

Now before you worry that I'm going to advocate we all wear dresses all the time or relinquish our right to vote and hold jobs at equal pay, let me explain where I'm going with this information. The Bible makes it very clear in Genesis 1 and 2 that God created women and men using different methods. He also created us, according to these same passages, to fulfill different jobs. He gave us very different bodies with different functions. We're just different. Men are masculine and women are feminine. The fact that we are both, male and female, created in His image indicates that men possess more profound doses of some of God's attributes while women possess others more consistently. For instance, men are *generally* more equipped to bear physical burdens, to fight battles requiring strength and stamina, to father (and all that entails), and to speak loudly. Women are *generally* more suited to speak with tenderness, to nurture, to create beauty, and to soothe. All of these traits, both those that are predominantly masculine and those considered more feminine, are characteristics of God which we see Him display throughout the course of His Word. He bears our heavy burdens, fights our battles, loves and disciplines us like a father, and speaks loudly to get our attention when necessary. He also loves us with tenderness, nurtures our gifts and abilities, creates a new sunrise every morning, and sooths us when we are distraught.

Let's look at some scriptures that show us God relating to us and to the world using both masculine and feminine character traits. Read the following passages in your Bible. Beside the scripture reference put an "F" if the verse reveals a "feminine" trait from our God, and an "M" if it shows a "masculine" trait. Keep in mind that these traits, while we may be labeling them feminine and masculine, are all *godly attributes* first. He created us in *His* image, not the other way around. You may want to write the character trait out to the right of the reference as well.

M/F	Scripture Reference	Trait
_____	Deuteronomy 1:30	_____
_____	Deuteronomy 1:31	_____
_____	Deuteronomy 1:32-33	_____
_____	Deuteronomy 8:3	_____
_____	2 Samuel 7:14	_____

_____	Psalm 18:1-2	_____
_____	Psalm 18:47	_____
_____	Psalm 23:5	_____
_____	Psalm 27:4	_____
_____	Psalm 29:4	_____
_____	Psalm 72:13	_____
_____	Psalm 103:8	_____
_____	Psalm 139:13-14	_____
_____	Psalm 147:3	_____
_____	Isaiah 40:11	_____
_____	Matthew 23:37	_____
_____	Hebrews 12:5-7	_____

We, male and female, were created in God's image. He created men to showcase some of His character traits more profoundly and women to display others more consistently.

Why did God create man and woman "in His own image"? We are His crowning creation. While He created the entire world for His enjoyment, He created man and woman to *glorify* Him. We're to reflect His character much like the moon reflects the sun's light. We're not supposed to be little gods, but we're supposed to point to the one true God through our character, words and actions. Basically, we're supposed to grow up to be just like our Father.

While women can often train their bodies to carry burdens and fight battles and men can possess the talents to create beautiful things and nurture the heart of a child, we still need to realize that it is in our respective feminine and masculine roles that we are more apt to glorify God in a way that draws others to the source of our light. You see, it isn't that as a woman I'm just automatically a great mom who knows how to be tender and soft with her children. I may have to pray a lot and seek God persistently in order to speak kindly to my children, nurture their growing minds and bodies, and comfort their broken hearts. God has created me for these tasks and He has made me feminine (whether I feel that way or not). But I will have to lean heavily on Him in order to do these feminine jobs well. And that is when I glorify God the best – when I fulfill my God-ordained female role, submitted to Him and dependent on Him for the strength, the wisdom, and the ability.

Do you see any benefit of a godly marriage where the husband is displaying his

masculine traits by God's grace and the wife is fulfilling her feminine calling in a

gracious way? If so, what are some of those benefits?

_____

_____

_____

_____

About this time I think I can hear some of you saying, "But wait a minute. I know a lot of women who don't *seem* especially feminine. They don't know how to do any of the feminine things like cook or sew or do hair. Did God make a mistake? Are these women supposed to squeeze into some uncomfortable role just because they're women?" Well, let's think about these things a minute. But let's commit to use God's Word as our standard while we do our thinking!

We know from Genesis 1 and 2 that God created us female, different from the male. Adam and Eve were created, from what we can tell in this same account, to complement each other, not to compete with each other. They were made to meet specific needs that the other had. They had different bodies with different abilities. They were given different tasks. **Now, what has changed since then? You tell me in the space below.**

The only thing that has really changed since Adam and Eve were first created and placed in that garden to glorify God and complement each other's lives is that sin entered the world and people began to drift away from God. Eventually, as our cultures drifted further and further from God's Word, people, specifically women, began to question why women weren't equal. Actually God had created men and women *equal* from the very beginning, but He also created women *uniquely* feminine with feminine roles. While some cultures abused and degraded women (and some still do), it was never God's intent for women to be seen as second class creatures. We know this to be true for at least several reasons. First, look at the creation of Eve. As God took a rib from Adam and created a woman from that rib, we see He had tenderness toward, purpose for, and satisfaction in that special creation. Secondly, Jesus, while He walked on this earth, consistently honored women, spoke to them, loved them, and offered them hope. Finally Galatians 3:28 says there is no distinction between male and female in Christ Jesus. We stand on even ground at the foot of the cross. God has not changed His estimation of woman, but He also has not changed His plans for woman (or man) since He first spelled out those plans to the first couple.

Perhaps the reason some women seem less feminine and some men seem less masculine is because we have strayed so far from biblical gender identities for so long that our lifestyles, our culture, and our worldviews make it harder for little boys and little girls to grow up knowing who they are and feeling comfortable with that identity. The feminist movement supposedly elevated women, but, in fact, it only degraded biblical womanhood in an effort to convince women to be more like men. God had already elevated women by giving them a divine purpose. Feminists essentially told women that being a woman was not enough. They devalued the roles that women are most comfortable in, most fulfilled in, and most needed in, so that women would instead take up the roles of men. They insisted that equality means sameness and argued that fulfilling different roles creates inequality. Now the generations birthed by those feminists are confused.

If we are going to teach our daughters and granddaughters how to fulfill God's biblical mandate for womanhood, we have our work cut out for us. We must go against the cultural tide and teach our daughters that God has a plan and that plan is a good, fulfilling, and honorable plan. First, many of us must allow God to convince us that this is true.

What feminine attributes and/or roles do you struggle with the most? _____

_____

_____

Which feminine attributes and/or roles do you most enjoy? In other words, what do you

like about being a woman? _____

_____

_____

What do you find confusing about being a woman in today's culture? This is your

opportunity to share any frustrations you may have about feeling pulled in two different

directions, etc. _____

_____

_____

_____

_____

_____

God's design for women transcends any particular role, though we do have roles to play. It goes beyond feminine characteristics such as soft hands, gentle touches, pretty hair, and sweet voices. God's plan for women, like it or not, is still the same one He gave to Eve in the garden. Over the next couple of days we'll learn each component of that plan and how we can carry it out with enthusiasm and grace in our current culture.

Looking Out From My Front Porch

Our country was one of the forerunners in adopting feminist views and values. While some may see that as a virtue, others would conclude that it has led to our demise. Check out this quote from the second president of the United States, John Adams:

> From all that I have read of history and government and
> human life and manners, I have drawn this conclusion: that
> the manners of women were the most infallible barometer
> to ascertain the degree of morality and virtue of a nation.
> The Jews, the Greeks, the Romans, the Swiss, the Dutch, all
> lost their public spirit and their republican forms of
> government when they lost the modesty and domestic virtues
> of their women. [1]

Now these words just reflect the opinion of one mortal man, not the estimation of God, but they certainly give us something to think about. Would you agree with Adams that the behavior of women so strongly affects the stability and prosperity of our culture? Explain why you do or do not agree with this theory.

Nancy Leigh DeMoss is the host and teacher for the *Revive Our Hearts* daily radio program for women, which is heard on over 250 stations. Single and never married, Nancy has a heart for helping women grasp and embrace God's Word, especially as it applies to their lives. She has written an excellent book entitled *Lies Women Believe and the Truths That Set Them Free* in which she explores many of the deceptions women have bought into in our culture. The back cover of her book *Biblical Womanhood* reads:

> The feminist revolution was supposed to bring women greater fulfillment and freedom. Yet many of us are feeling anything but fulfilled and free. Across generational lines, inside the church and out, we are understanding that we have lost the beauty and wonder of our distinctive makeup and calling as women. We are realizing that what was supposed to lift us up has been tearing down society, churches, and most importantly, our own families.[2]

What would you say is the result of our culture embracing the feministic movement? _____

_____

_____

_____

Leaving My Front Porch

Dear friend, I fear that many of us, including myself, have drifted far from the biblical pattern for womanhood. Just saying those words, "biblical womanhood", I get kind of a bad taste in my mouth. I'm just being honest here. For me this is where the rubber meets the road. I'll talk with you all day long about the biblical stance on abortion, sex outside of marriage, homosexuality, law suits, entertainment standards, etc. But when you start talking biblical womanhood you've gone to meddling in my business. You know what I mean?

Let's commit to approaching the rest of this study with humility and teachable spirits. We're going to need them, ladies. I know what's coming in the next few days and it's not all fun blanks to fill in and matching games. But you hang in there with me, let God speak, and when we're through, we'll all go get pedicures. We're going to need them after our toes have been stepped on so many times!

Day 2 – Not *Just* a Helper

Reading on My Front Porch

Read: Genesis 2:15-25 in your Bible. After God had created Adam, placed him in the garden and given him his marching orders, He acknowledged that it wasn't good for Adam to be alone. What did God say Adam needed?

Visiting on My Front Porch

The first role given to woman is the role of *helper*. As unfulfilling as that may sound right now let's give it a chance. Let's explore this role a little further before we shake our fist at God and declare, "That's not good enough for me. I have a better idea." Prayerfully and humbly think through the following questions.

Specifically what kind of helper did God want to find for Adam? _____

What tasks had God given Adam that he might need help with? (See Genesis 1: 26-30;

2:15) _____

_____

_____

Read 1 Corinthians 11:8-9. These verses may rattle your bones a little and put you on edge,

but honestly, do they back up what we read in Genesis 2? _____

How? _____

God determined that it was not good for Adam to be alone, so He created a helper for him. Already we see that it was not God's intention for men and women to operate independently of one another, in competition with each other, or in different directions. They were to work toward the same goals, in harmony and cooperation, but each would have different tasks and roles. Genesis 2:15 implies that Adam was given the job of manager and later Eve was given the assignment of helping him with that task. No one else and nothing else could fill Eve's shoes (if she had had any!).

As we determined yesterday, God has not changed His purpose for women at any point in history. He has given some women some awesome gifts, talents, opportunities, and tasks, but His purpose has never changed. Woman, like man, is to bring God glory by accurately reflecting the nature of God. One of the ways she is to do that, in a broad sense, is by helping her husband. John Piper clarifies this unique feminine purpose well by writing, "At the heart of mature femininity is a freeing disposition to affirm, receive, and nurture strength and leadership from worthy men in ways appropriate to a woman's differing relationships."[3]

While marriage may be the primary relationship in which a married woman is to exercise this role, women also have opportunity to be of help to men in a variety of appropriate relationships, as suggested by Piper in the quote above. Single and married women have the opportunity to be helpers to various men God puts in their lives such as an employer or pastor. When a woman gives encouragement, lends insight, exercises faith, serves with generosity, lends a helping hand, or provides support to a man with whom she has an appropriate relationship, she creates an environment in which he can be his best and do what he is called to do. Being a helper in such a relationship is not a subservient role, but a necessary role that causes the job to get done in a productive and God-glorifying way. The role of helper is not reduced to only mopping floors and ironing shirts either. There are multitudes of ways women help the men in their lives accomplish tasks every day. Whether you are a teacher, a doctor, an engineer, a homemaker, or a clerical assistant, you can be a helper. In fact, the role of helper is not so much tied to your occupation. It is an attitude of love, service, and sacrifice that permeates everything you do and are.

If you are married, what are some of the ways you currently and consistently help your husband? _____

_____

_____

_____

If you are married, what are some additional ways you could help your husband from this point on? _____

_____

_____

What men, besides a husband, has God placed in your life that you have the opportunity to help? _____

_____

Explain some of the appropriate ways you can be helpful to a male employer, family member, pastor, or organization leader. _____

_____

_____

_____

Now let's just tap into our womanly intuition and think a bit. Why do you believe a woman's help makes such a difference in a man's life? _____

_____

_____

_____

Conversely, what are some of the things women do that *do not help* men? What are some of the detrimental things you or others have done to men, causing them to struggle in their roles? _____

_____

_____

So what exactly are we women supposed to help our men do? Just like Eve was supposed to help Adam carry out God's orders in taking care of the garden, ruling over the animals and subduing the earth, *we are supposed to help the men in our lives be obedient to God.* But Eve messed up and caused her man to sin instead. Our task is to encourage and help our husbands, sons, fathers, brothers, employers, spiritual leaders, and organizational leaders to obey God's Word and will for their lives. We can best do that by praying for them and knowing God's Word for ourselves, something Eve neglected to do.

Read Proverbs 31:10-31 in your Bible. What word is used to describe this woman in verse

10?_____

When I read over the description of the Proverbs 31 woman one of the things that strikes me most is that she seems to be a very *capable* woman. She knows how to run a home, sew clothes, trade in the marketplace, work a business deal, and invest her earnings. She also knows how to make her husband and children feel secure, loved, and happy. I don't think she just happened to be born knowing all these things. I think she studiously learned her trade, followed the examples of wise women before her, honed her craft, and took good care of herself so she could help her husband from a place of strength, ability, and confidence.

Sometimes we might think of a helper as one who isn't capable of doing something on their own so, therefore, they are relegated to the task of helper. Such a person might simply be there for moral support, good company, or menial tasks. But that's not the kind of helper it appears God created us to be as wives. The Proverbs 31 wife certainly was no trophy wife. She was smart, informed, confident, competent, strong, and capable. And her husband sang her praises.

Instead of complaining because we have been given the task of helping our husbands, let's take the role seriously and do everything we can to make ourselves the strongest, wisest, most capable, and most confident women possible, so we can excel at our role. I'm not advocating being pushy, demanding, bossy, controlling, or a know-it-all, mind you. The Scriptures give fair warning about such a demeanor.

Read the following Proverbs and note how the women in these verses are described.

Proverbs 9:13   _____

Proverbs 11:22   _____

Proverbs 21:9   _____

Proverbs 21:19   _____

Proverbs 27:15   _____

No, I don't want to be a wife that is overbearing and contentious. Being a helper can be a tricky position to be in. I need to know when to speak, when to be quiet. I must learn to gauge my husband's receptiveness to my ideas and encouragements. And I have to know how my man works, what sits well with him, and what agitates him. But I can best help my man when I am physically strong, emotionally stable, spiritually full, and adequately knowledgeable about the tasks I need to accomplish. Let's commit to helping from a place of strength, ability, and confidence.

One more thing, and this is a biggy. I've been saving this final point for those of you who still may not be convinced that there is great worth in being a helper.

Read the following scriptures in your Bible and match them with the corresponding type of help mentioned on the right.

A. 1 Samuel 7:11-13	_____	delivers me from the adversary
B. Psalm 42:11	_____	picks me up when I'm pushed
C. Psalm 54:4	_____	keeps me from fearing people
D. Psalm 60:11	_____	increases my faith
E. Psalm 118:13	_____	subdues my enemies
F. Isaiah 41:10	_____	gives hope/lifts my countenance
G. Mark 9:24	_____	strengthens me and holds me up
H. John 14:16	_____	sustains my soul
I. John 14:26	_____	stays with me forever
J. Hebrews 13:6	_____	teaches me all things

Now, who provides all this help? Who is this mighty helper? _____

We have a great example of how to be a helper. God is our ever present Helper. He is the Almighty God of this universe, the sovereign King, the omnipotent Lord, but He does not ever mind coming to our assistance. Ah, indeed, what is man that such a God is even mindful of him, much less that He is willing to be our Helper? If God is willing to stoop down to help us shouldn't we be honored to help others?

Looking Out From My Front Porch

When I first discovered that one of my primary functions as a woman is to be a helper to my husband and other men, I bristled. I knew Genesis said that was why God created woman, but surely he had made a few amendments to His original purpose statement. Alas, I am now convinced that being a helper is one of my most important God-appointed roles. And now that I think about it, I do a lot of helping already. I've just preferred to call it something a little more self-elevating. In fact, in the last several decades many women have resorted to re-titling their jobs in order to feel better about them. We've gone from being housewives to homemakers to domestic engineers. We've stopped being secretaries and become administrative assistants. Teachers are now educators and teachers' aids are paraprofessionals. Whatever. Ladies, let's get real. God made us to be helpers, so let's embrace that role, make no apologies about it, and do it well. I want to fulfill God's purpose for me and I don't need to rename it in some lame attempt to justify my life to the world. He created me and gave me a wonderful, necessary purpose. If I accept it, embrace it, do it, and excel at it, then I'll find joy and contentment in it.

Barbara Hughes writes in her book *Disciplines of a Godly Woman,*

> So why does our blood pressure rise at the mention
> of the word *helper*? It's a cultural norm for us to
> associate weakness and even inferiority with the one
> who assists. No one wants to play second fiddle. But
> the fact is, without a second violin there is no
> harmony.[4]

How can you help other women understand, accept, embrace and fulfill the role of

helper? _____

_____

_____

How can we teach young girls that there is value and reward in being a helper? _____

_____

_____

Leaving My Front Porch

Today's lesson may have been a little hard for you to swallow; it was for me. Perhaps you're still working on getting it down. Keep swallowing, Sister! Treat yourself to a Diet Coke or cappuccino if it'll help. And ask God to help you see the glory of His purpose. He is not trying to make a fool of you, demean you, or relegate you to some second class position. He loves you and has created you for a truly noble calling.

In fact, it is in serving that we are most like our Savior. Remember how He washed the feet of His disciples and told them to serve each other in the same way? I've never had to wash my husband's feet, but the truth is that while I haven't yet, I may need to one day. Some of you already have needed to bathe your husband, spoon feed him, sit patiently beside his bedside, and wipe his brow. Some of you have already buried your dear husbands and would give anything to be able to serve him today. Bless your sweet hearts. You have fulfilled your purpose well. May God grant each of us the ability to see the blessing that comes in helping another to live well.

Day 3 – Making a Happy Home

Reading on My Front Porch

Read: Genesis 4:1-2 in your Bible. What did Eve say when she gave birth to her first son, Cain? What thoughts do you think went through her mind with the occurrence of this miracle?

Visiting on My Front Porch

Today we're actually going to try to look at two roles God has given woman to fulfill. They are intertwined, but not completely dependent upon one another. The first role is that of *nurturer*. The second is *homemaker*. Do not dismiss either of these roles if you are not married or if you are childless. You will soon learn that all women were created to fill these roles to one extent or another.

We Are Made to Nurture

Women are created to be life-bearers. Our bodies were built to conceive, carry, bear, and care for new life. In fact our bodies prepare themselves repeatedly for this privilege and responsibility. Never is a woman more feminine than when she embraces each stage of this life-giving cycle. Of course, because we live in a fallen world that is marred by sin, some women are not able to conceive or bear children. That is not a reflection of God's attitude toward that particular woman, but simply one of the unfortunate results of living outside the Garden of Eden. Still, every woman has the potential and opportunity to nurture young lives, whether physically, emotionally, intellectually or spiritually. Because that is part of God's assignment for women, we need to take the role of nurturer seriously and commit to it.

Read Proverbs 31:15, 21, 26-28. According to these scriptures, what kind of priority does the virtuous woman give to nurturing her children? _____

_____

What are some of the ways she cares for them? _____

_____

Now read the rest of Proverbs 31:10-31. What are some of the other activities this woman is involved in that could prevent her from making her children a priority? _____

_____

_____

_____

How do you think this woman manages to give her children priority and still do so many other things? The answer is woven into the passage. _____

_____

_____

_____

Did you notice that the woman rises while it is still dark to feed her family (vs. 15)? Did you also notice that she is prepared for the cold months of the winter because she has planned ahead and made or purchased adequate clothing for her family (vs. 21)? Perhaps you also noticed that she is able to teach her children wisdom because she has first acquired wisdom from God (vs. 26). This woman is not idle, but industrious, and she puts great effort into caring for her family (vs. 27). While the Proverbs 31 woman often intimidates us, she really should inspire us. She shows us that being a woman is no small task, but requires thought, planning, effort, and enthusiasm. She teaches us to prioritize, too. She shows us that while we *may* have a career outside the home (vs. 16), enjoy hobbies (vs. 13), exercise to keep fit (vs. 17), put a little effort into our physical appearance (vs. 22), and serve in the community (vs. 20) we should never neglect our family by getting overly caught up in other pursuits. Family comes first.

What do you think are some possible characteristics that show up in a home where the

mother makes nurturing the family her priority? _____

_____

_____

What are some possible effects in the home if a mother makes her career, hobbies,

ministries, or other pursuits her priority instead of her family? _____

_____

_____

Which household of the two looks most like your household? _____

Why? _____

_____

What are some ways that you make nurturing your family a priority? _____

_____

_____

What are some ways that you have neglected your family and that you need to improve

by making them more of a priority? _____

_____

_____

Ladies, remember even single women and those with no children in the home have an obligation to nurture young lives. Especially today, there are so many children, teenagers, and young women who need mentors to help them set their feet on the right path. Because many women have been duped by the promises of the feminist movement, many families are left uncared for. Children are raising themselves, whether their mothers are absent from the home for long hours while they work or whether they are simply too exhausted to mother with the energy required to do the job right. Divorce and single parenting have also taken a toll on the family and left many children without the support they need at home. While many single moms certainly do their best to provide financially for their families while also nurturing them at home, most single moms testify that the responsibility leaves them weary and frustrated. Many such moms would welcome the help of a humble and gracious woman willing to come alongside and love her children. Finally, many mothers (and fathers) have simply not counted the cost of raising children and refuse to do the job well out of selfishness and self-centeredness. While some abuse and harm their children, many more simply neglect them. We have more than one generation of young people who are searching for love, support, and attention from somebody who will make them feel significant and hopeful. Women who know the love of God, have experienced the redeeming power of Jesus, and have the Holy Spirit working within them are the best candidates for making a difference in the lives of these wounded souls.

I have a dear friend whose own nest is almost empty. With two daughters in college and one very independent son finishing up his last year in high school, Kim has turned much of her attention to nurturing other children and teenagers. She gives rides to and from church to teens whose own parents will not or cannot bring them. She and a friend lead a teen girls' Bible study on Sunday evenings that is full of teenagers whose parents are not Christians. And, with their parents' permission, she counsels teenagers who are struggling with problems at home, in school, and in relationships. One might think that what Kim does is simply icing on the cake, extra. But in fact, if Kim didn't drive some of these students to church or teach some of these teen girls about how to be a godly young woman, no one would. In many cases, she is the only Christian woman with whom these young people have a growing, healthy, and purposeful relationship. Her nurturing of these children is crucial and beneficial to the kingdom of God. There really is no higher calling when you think about it.

Reread Proverbs 31:20. How does the Proverbs 31 woman nurture those outside of her

home?_____

_____

Now read Titus 2:3-5. What responsibility does the "older woman" have for nurturing

others according to this passage? _____

_____

What character traits does the older woman need to develop in order to carry out this

responsibility well? _____

_____

Who is the older woman? How old is she? What do you think? _____

_____

Are you an older woman? Explain your answer and be ready to share it with others. _____

_____

Are you presently nurturing anyone? Your own children? Other people's children? Young

women? _____

In what way are you nurturing them? _____

_____

_____

Today I got a surprise e-mail from a high school girlfriend I have not seen or talked with in years. Lee shared with me a little about her life in her brief note and I can tell you without hesitation that this is one enthusiastic, beautiful and godly woman. Lee and her husband have been married for 25 years, but they never had any children. Still, without having talked with me, mind you, she supplied just the story I needed for this portion of our Bible study. Lee has been a consultant for the BeautiControl® skincare company for about three and a half years. But she's made her endeavor with BeautiControl® more than just a profit-turning career. She's used it to nurture young women just like God intended her to. Here's a snippet of her e-mail to me:

> I've got a team of about 70 women, with about 10 of those really working to advance in their careers and realize their dreams/goals in life. I look at it as my ministry and have a passion for helping to empower women and, hopefully along the way, if they aren't already a Christ-follower, to point them in that direction or at the very least be a witness for them along their journey through their involvement with BeautiControl®. My "ministry" extends to my clients, who I initially have at a spa party...it's so cool to have women show up for what they think is just another home party but leave feeling pampered and relaxed. So many women don't get to feel too special in their lives since they're busy giving to everyone else in their families, so if I can make them feel special for just a little while, the smiles and feelings of "aaaahhhh", and a heartfelt "thank you" as they leave, is hugely rewarding.

Lee may not have children at home to call her own, but surely God is pleased with this woman who takes seriously the mandate to nurture life. Well done, Lee.

Ladies, never underestimate the responsibility to nurture your children. It is perhaps your greatest privilege and highest calling. It may also require your greatest effort, sacrifice, and time on your knees. But in the end, nothing is more rewarding than helping someone grow up to be all God meant them to be. Whether the subject of your nurturing is your own child, a neglected or hurting child, a student in your classroom, a healthcare patient or a young woman who needs to be mentored, embrace the role God has given you to pour life into an impressionable young mind and heart. Poet William Ross Wallace expressed beautifully how important this God-given role is.

The Hand That Rocks the Cradle Is the Hand That Rules the World

Blessings on the hand of women!
Angels guard its strength and grace,
In the palace, cottage, hovel,
Oh, no matter where the place;
Would that never storms assailed it,
Rainbows ever gently curled;
For the hand that rocks the cradle
Is the hand that rules the world.

Infancy's the tender fountain,
Power may with beauty flow,
Mother's first to guide the streamlets,
From them souls unresting grow--
Grow on for the good or evil,
Sunshine streamed or evil hurled;
For the hand that rocks the cradle
Is the hand that rules the world.

Woman, how divine your mission
Here upon our natal sod!
Keep, oh, keep the young heart open
Always to the breath of God!
All true trophies of the ages
Are from mother-love impearled;
For the hand that rocks the cradle
Is the hand that rules the world.

Blessings on the hand of women!
Fathers, sons, and daughters cry,
And the sacred song is mingled
With the worship in the sky--
Mingles where no tempest darkens,
Rainbows evermore are hurled;
For the hand that rocks the cradle
Is the hand that rules the world.

We Are Called to Care for the Home

Both Proverbs 31 and Titus 2:3-5 indicate that women are to care for the affairs of the household. Domesticity – devotion to the quality of home life – is a God-ordained role for which women are equipped and suited. As we mentioned on the first day of this study of biblical womanhood, if some women *seem* or *feel* less suited for the domestic roles, it is not so much because they were born ill-equipped. It is more likely because we have lost the art and the urgency of passing down domestic skills and, perhaps even more importantly, a love for things domestic. We have minimized this role in our culture, relegated it to someone else when possible, and neglected to teach our daughters how to care for their homes. In fact, many in our culture have just opted to leave many tasks undone because those jobs are unpleasant, time-consuming, or laborious.

Perhaps women have no one to blame more than themselves for making domestic jobs seem trivial, distasteful, and demeaning. Instead of taking care of our homes with passion, enthusiasm, creativity, and love, we've begrudgingly provided for our families and cared for our homes by picking up fast food for dinner, cleaning minimally, and completely neglecting some jobs such as ironing, sewing, and gardening. We've bought into the bad press given to domesticity and, therefore, we've found little fulfillment in the associated tasks. By the time the feminist movement had washed over this country like dirty bath water, women had developed a disdain for all things domestic. If a woman dared to claim that she enjoyed taking care of her home, she was considered silly, ignorant, unsophisticated, and behind the times.

Fortunately the 90s and the 21st century have ushered in a renewed zeal for domestic pursuits. Martha Stewart has taught us that creating a gracious home can be "a good thing." *Taste of Home* magazine provides women with recipes that remind them of foods their mothers made. Pampered Chef has brought families back to the dinner table and the Food Network has made cooking fun and hip. Indeed our country seems to have embraced the art of domesticity once again and elevated the associated tasks to the level of an art form. But ladies, here's the key. We need to realize once and for all that taking care of a home well is a valid, honorable, worthy, and important responsibility that requires hard work, creativity, enthusiasm, intelligence, and skill, not because our fickle culture deems it so, but because God made it so.

While the first priority of caring for the home is tending to and nurturing the people of your home, it is also vital for women to heed God's call to make the physical environment of that home a pleasant one. When we take the time to keep our homes clean, well-organized, fresh, and warmly decorated, our families have a place to rest, regroup, retreat, and re-energize. They have a place in which to thrive.

Lest you think home environment is no big deal, keep in mind that the Bible reveals it to be a big deal to God on several accounts. Read the following scriptures in your Bible. In the space provided record what home is mentioned and God's relationship to that home. You might also give a few of the biblical words used to describe the atmosphere of that home.

Scripture	Home	Biblical Description
Genesis 2:8-17	_____	_____
		_____
Genesis 17:1-8	_____	_____
		_____
Exodus 3:8	_____	_____
		_____
John 14:2-3	_____	_____
		_____
Revelation 21	_____	_____
		_____

God is all about making a nice home for His people. He set Adam and Eve up in a perfect garden home from the very beginning. He intended for them to live in perfect harmony with Him there. He led His chosen people to a land flowing with milk and honey where He intended for them to find rest, blessing, and a safe haven. Jesus is now preparing for us a mansion in heaven. He tells us to lay our treasure up there instead of here on earth because that is our eternal home. And Revelation 21 gives us a glimpse of that home – a place beautifully illumined by the glory of God.

We've established already that our primary purpose in life is to reflect well on our God, to glorify Him in all we do and say. When we, as women, put in the effort and time required to make a warm, inviting, restful, and lovely home for our family, we reflect our God's desire and ability to provide a lovely home for us. We reflect His creativity, His warmth, His grace, and His beauty.

When we care for our homes by decorating, cleaning, repairing, and adding our individual touches, we show our family members love. We also give them a haven in which they can grow, rest, laugh, learn, receive nourishment, and find safety. And we are able to provide biblical hospitality for those to whom we minister through our home. In fact, for a woman, the primary place for our ministry should be our home. That is where we can best help our husbands, nurture our children, teach younger women, and extend a gracious hand to the hurting.

What is your greatest struggle in working at home? _____

_____

_____

_____

What is your greatest strength in working at home? (Do you do a good job preparing

tasty, nutritious meals? Have you decorated with warmth and good taste? Do you keep

your house especially clean?...) _____

_____

_____

What five words would your family members use to describe your home (not your house,

but your home)? Ask them if you dare! _____

_____

What do you think you need to do better, more often, more regularly, or differently to

make your home a better place for your family to thrive? _____

_____

_____

Contributing author Carolyn Mahaney writes in *Biblical Womanhood*:

> Proverbs 14:1 says, "The wise woman builds
> her house, but with her own hands the foolish one
> tears hers down." In other words, the home is our
> place to build. Our culture says it's not a place
> worthy of our best labors, but we have to be careful
> not to allow the world to affect our thinking. The
> home is our primary place for ministry…Our scope
> of ministry is different than that of men, but it is no
> less important: It is God's assignment for us.[5]

Looking Out From My Front Porch

If we are going to pass down to the next generation of young women a more biblical approach to caring for our families and homes, we have our work cut out for us. While the Food Network, The Learning Channel, and Home and Garden TV may be on our side, our culture as a whole still smirks at those who put too much energy, passion, and time into domestic pursuits. We're going to have to swim against the current and show our girls that God's call to invest in the home is fun, challenging, rewarding, and crucial.

If you have a daughter, granddaughter or daughter-in-law, what are some ways you can

pass down a biblical approach to family and home life?_____

_____

_____

_____

_____

Leaving My Front Porch

Sometimes we minimize those responsibilities and duties that we feel unprepared for, uninterested in, or distracted from. For instance, if it's been a while since I've cleaned my floors, I may rationalize my neglect by saying something like, "Well I think it's more important to spend time playing outside with my children than to clean all the time." Let's get real. No one's suggesting I need to clean *all the time*. Neither is anyone buying the idea that I play outside with my children 'round the clock! The fact is I don't feel like mopping and vacuuming.

If we've been making excuses because we've neglected to nurture our children or tend to our homes, let's put an end to that today. I know I need to do a better job with both of these monumental tasks, and I can tell you exactly what excuses I allow to feed my neglect. But I want to please my God. I don't want to buy into the world's deception that says a woman can only find great worth and meaning by pursuing her own goals and dreams. I want to adopt God's goal for me and do it to the best of my ability.

Let's close with a prayer of commitment today. I'm committing to prioritizing my day so that I can properly nurture my children physically, emotionally, and spiritually. I also commit to putting aside the excuses I've accumulated that keep me from working around my house. In fact, I'm going to go clean a few toilets right after I get up off my knees!

Day 4 – A Choice?

Reading on My Front Porch

Read: Psalm 139 in your Bible. According to verse 16, what has God seen that no other eyes have seen? According to the same scripture, at what point did God begin to write your story in His book?

Visiting on My Front Porch

Today we're taking a little bit of a departure from the theme of biblical womanhood, but, then again, not really.

We've already established that women were created to conceive, carry, bear, and nurture children. This is perhaps one of the greatest responsibilities of womanhood as well as one of the most wonderful blessings. But, unfortunately, our culture has brought another element to this phenomenal gift and role – that of life-ender. You may have already guessed that today we will take a necessary look at the abortion issue.

While abortion may seem to be more of a cultural hot topic than a biblical womanhood issue, it is in fact *women* who are choosing to end the lives of unborn children. This is a "choice" that our culture has insisted on giving to women, so I would be amiss to skip over this topic in a Bible study about developing a biblical worldview from a female perspective. Whether you are the mother of a young girl who could potentially get pregnant out of wedlock, an unmarried woman with her future ahead of her, a mother who thinks she has all the children she can handle, or a woman who has had an abortion in the past, this lesson is for you. It is for all of us who have female friends, family members, and co-workers whom we influence. It is for all of us who vote. It is for all of us who, at the insistence of our culture, have a choice.

Before we get too far in this lesson, let me remind us all that "there is therefore now no condemnation for those who are in Christ Jesus." (Romans 8:1) If you have had an abortion in the past, this lesson is not meant to bring guilt or judgment to you. While I believe the Bible clearly directs us to protect and value life, thus warning against abortion or any other act that would end a life prematurely, we need to understand that having an abortion is not the "worst sin" or an unpardonable offense. Ending a life is a serious matter and undoubtedly the God-fearing woman who has had an abortion will not rest peaceably until she has confessed that sin to her God, received His forgiveness through the death of Jesus Christ, and appropriated that pardon in her life. But once that issue has been dealt with by a woman and her God, no one has the right to place that burden of guilt back on those freed shoulders. Sweet sister, please know that I am not trying to load you down afresh with this lesson. The goal here is to examine this issue from a biblical viewpoint so that we as women can make right choices in the future and influence our world to see life in the womb as valuable and worthy of protection. Those of you who have had abortions have the added opportunity to speak the truth and defend the unborn from a platform of experience. Once you have healed enough and matured in God's grace, I encourage you to consider using that platform to speak the truth about this issue to our world.

There are two individuals most intimately involved in an abortion: the woman and the baby she carries in her womb. We'll begin our study by looking at this issue from the perspective of the growing life inside the woman, and then we'll consider things from the woman's vantage point. But we'll complete the study by looking at this growing miracle called life from the Creator's view point.

The Baby

Referring back to Psalm 139, how does the baby in the womb develop? (vs. 13) _____

_____

Though we depend on sonograms to see and detect the existence of a thriving baby, when

does God see it? (vs. 15) _____

When does this child's life begin? (vs. 16) _____

_____

Does this child already have a *purpose* when it is still in its mother's womb? (vs. 16) _____

What phrase indicates this? _____

     Psalm 139 and other scriptures such as Psalm 119:73 indicate that God is still intimately involved in the formation of each person. You see, He didn't just create Adam and Eve, but He forms each of us with His loving and artful hands. Each human life is a masterpiece created by the God of this universe to have a purpose, an impact, and an eternal spirit. He treasures each one and makes no mistakes.

The Woman

     Most people in favor of giving women the option of abortion argue that women have the right to control their own bodies. They contend that if the fetus (or baby) is growing in the woman, that woman should have the right to end that growth. Actually, they're partially correct. Women should have the right to control their bodies, but those rights, like all other personal rights, have limitations.

     As Americans we enjoy many rights – the right to free speech, the right to a free press, the right to practice a religion of choice, etc. But each of these rights is limited when the exercise of that freedom would adversely affect another person or group. For instance, I am free to express my opinion and say whatever I would like. But I can't shout "fire!" in a crowded movie theater where there is no fire without paying the penalty because my freely expressed speech would cause a throng of people to hurt themselves trying to leave the theater in a rush. In the same way, I am free to practice whatever religion I would like. But if that religion involves me sacrificing 16-year-old virgins at the mouth of a volcano in Hawaii, I will be arrested and prosecuted. My freely practiced religion would adversely affect those 16-year-old virgins, to say the least. My personal freedoms are limited when they adversely affect anyone else.

Read Romans 14:7 in your Bible. Write the verse in the space provided.

     When a woman chooses to end a life she is making a choice that adversely affects that life growing within her body. She is ending a life that God began. She is "living for herself" and harming another life that God cherishes.

The Creator
Read the scriptures below and complete the statements that tell us about God's
relationship with life. Choose from the words listed here to complete the sentences.

protect   created   womb

Death   gives   victorious   abundant

Genesis 1:27   God _____life.

Exodus 20:13; 21:12   God put forth laws to _____ life.

Luke 1:39-42   God recognized life in the _____.

John 10:10   God wants us to have _____ life in Jesus.

Acts 17:24-28   God _____ life and sets the boundaries of our

                         existence.

1 Corinthians 15:55-57   _____ is the enemy, but Jesus is _____ over

                         death.

        While an abortion may seem like the only feasible decision to a woman who has
mistakenly gotten pregnant, it is never right to end a life that God has begun. And though
a woman who has conceived a child through a rape or incest may agonize over the life that
is growing within her, ending that life will not end her pain. It will, in fact, only add to it.
God has promised to walk with us through every crisis in life. He will walk especially
close to the one who honors Him by carrying a new life to term, even when it is not easy
for her.

A Nation
        Not only is abortion a wrong choice for a woman because it infringes upon the life
of an innocent child, it is also a choice that is detrimental to a nation.

Read 2 Kings 17:13-18, 30-31 in your Bible.

        The people of Israel had stiffened their necks and rebelled against God. They built
idols similar to the ones worshipped by the neighboring nations and began to worship them
in pagan rituals, including the sacrifice of children to the fire. What was God's reaction to
this behavior according to 2 Kings 17:18? Check all the answers that apply.

    O   He blessed them with prosperity.

    O   He protected them from adversity.

    O   He was very angry with them.

    O   He removed them from His sight.

    O   He blessed them with fruitful wombs.

It is estimated that there have been over 40 million abortions performed in the United States since the landmark case of Roe vs. Wade legalized abortions in this country. While we may like to believe there have been no serious ramifications from this murderous behavior, perhaps we should think again. Women in the United States are facing fertility difficulties like never before. "According to the Centers for Disease Control and Prevention (CDC), the number of couples who report difficulty becoming pregnant or carrying a pregnancy to term has grown from 6.1 million in 1995 to 7.3 million in 2002."[6] Also, surprisingly America has gone from being a nation with one of the lowest infant mortality rates to having one of the highest among industrialized, modern nations.[7] Each year more than 28,000 newborns die in this country.[8] While politicians worry that this mind-boggling statistic indicates Americans are not getting sufficient bang for their medical bucks, I'm wondering if God is not trying to get our attention or, worse yet, if He is disciplining us for not only allowing, but providing, funding, and promoting, abortions. While no one really wants to think about God bringing judgment on our country for the millions of abortions that have been performed here, could it be that, as in 2 Kings 17:18, God has turned His face from us?

Proverbs 14:34 says, "Righteousness exalts a nation, but sin is a disgrace to any people." In Deuteronomy 28 God outlines for His people the blessings He will bring upon them if they "diligently obey" Him, but He also describes in some detail the curses they will encounter if they turn aside from Him.

Read Deuteronomy 28:15-19 in your Bible.

What does Deuteronomy 28:18 indicate to you? _____

_____

_____

Keep in mind that this scripture is not to be applied to individual cases of infertility. Instead it indicates that the *nation* that turns away from God and His standard for righteousness could incur a greater incidence of infertility and infant mortality. God can bless the wombs of a nation and He can remove that blessing.

Looking Out From My Front Porch

What can you and I do to help women make a better choice when they find themselves in a crisis pregnancy situation? What can we do to help our nation turn back to God by valuing the life in the womb? Do we really need to do anything?

While those who work in prolife organizations struggle to make changes in legislation, convince women to give birth to their babies, and change the mindset of a perverse generation, the church is largely just standing by like baffled spectators. Those who are on the frontlines often lament that the church has done little to get involved in a situation that is so obviously an affront to a holy God. Perhaps it is time that you and I did more to help.

I'm including a list of both simple and more involved ways in which we can make a difference in the abortion issue. Please look over this list prayerfully, asking God to spark within you an interest, a passion, and a calling. Put a check beside any of the ideas that you could follow through with. Then prayerfully commit to making that phone call, doing that research, writing that letter or whatever you have chosen to do. As women who have been given a "choice," let's make the right one, and let's help our nation to make the right one as well.

_____ **Pray** – for doctors who perform abortions, legislators, women in crisis

_____ **Educate yourself** – about current legislation, about fetal development, about abortions, about the work done at crisis pregnancy centers, about Planned Parenthood's agendas

_____ **Take a stand and be firm** – at work, among friends, with family, at parties

_____ **Support prolife groups** – Focus on the Family, local crisis pregnancy centers, etc.

_____ **Contact your legislators** – urge them to vote prolife and against abortion funding

_____ **Protest** – it's not for everyone, but someone needs to, with gentleness and respect

_____ **Help a crisis pregnancy center** – volunteer your time, get trained, supply diapers

_____ **Love those looking for hope** – those who've had abortions, those contemplating one

Life is not really just a woman's issue; it is a God issue. He is the giver of life and it is so precious to Him that He would pay the ultimate price in order to redeem our lost lives. But our culture has made new life and abortion a woman's choice. They have put the decision to let live or let die in the hands of millions of women. Ladies, we need to be a voice for life. Let's lift our voices and be heard.

Leaving My Front Porch

Pray with me today for the opportunity to be a light in a dark world. It won't be easy. Our culture has embraced abortions like they've embraced garbage disposals – just a modern convenience that takes care of one of life's unfortunate messes. That's a shame. Literally, a shame. We really need to pray.

Day 5 – Beauty Beyond Lipstick

Reading on My Front Porch

Read: 1 Peter 3:3-5 in your Bible. According to this passage, how did the holy women of former times make themselves beautiful?

Visiting on My Front Porch

Today we bring our study on developing a biblical worldview to a close. While it may seem a little anticlimactic to end such a broad and culturally significant study by looking at the topic of beauty, I think we're ending with just the exclamation mark many of us women need. Our world's view of what makes a woman beautiful has gone from extreme to dangerous in recent decades. Actually our world has always pushed the beauty meter to unhealthy extremes by using guilt, unhealthy role models, poor self-esteem, and envy to cajole women into aiming for unattainable and unrealistic beauty standards. Author Robin Marantz Henig provides insight on the long history of this obsession with physical appearance:

> Over the centuries, women have mauled and manipulated just about every body part—lips, eyes, ears, waists, skulls, foreheads, feet—that did not quite fit into the cookie-cutter ideal of a particular era's fashion. In China, almost up until World War II, upper-class girls had their feet bound, crippling them for life but ensuring the three- or four-inch-long feet that were prized as exquisitely feminine. In central Africa, the Mangbettu wrapped the heads of female infants in pieces of giraffe hide to attain the elongated, cone-shaped heads that were taken to be a sign of beauty and intelligence. During the Renaissance, well-born European women plucked out hairs, one by one, from the natural hairlines all the way back to the crown of their heads, to give themselves the high, rounded foreheads thought beautiful at the time....
>
> Among the Padaung people of early-twentieth-century Burma, the ideal of female beauty involved a greatly elongated neck, preferably fifteen inches or more. This was accomplished by fitting girls with a series of brass neck rings. At a very young age, girls began by wearing five rings; by the time they were fully grown they were wearing as many as twenty-four, piled one on top of another....
>
> The weight of the rings leads to crushed collarbones and broken ribs, and the vertebrae in the neck become stretched and floppy. Indeed, these women wear rings round-the-clock because, without them, their stretched-out necks are too weak to support their heads.[9]

While the examples from this historical sketch may seem extreme and dangerous even to us, some of our own modern beauty treatments are not much safer or more humane. Let's face it; we women go to great extremes to look beautiful.

What are some of the beauty treatments you use, do, or have done to you that, when you really think about it, are a little painful and humiliating? _____

_____

_____

Now sweet sister, if you didn't put at least one or two things on those blanks you go right back to that last question and think a little harder! I don't know very many women who don't sit patiently through one beauty regimen or another that they wish they could do without. We may love the results, but the process can be plain out painful! I've had more perms, color jobs, foil highlights, manicures, pedicures, dental treatments and piercings than I care to number, and I didn't enjoy the process of any of them. No ma'am, I don't even enjoy manicures! I love the way my nails look after a professional treatment, but I don't like having my cuticles trimmed or pushed back and I hate sitting with my hands under the drier for 15 long minutes. It's hard work being a woman! Amen?

I remember the first time I had my hair highlighted using "the cap." If you have no idea what I'm talking about, count your blessings. The beautician stuffed my big head and my massive amount of long, shoulder-length hair under a stretchy, rubber cap that was much smaller and tighter than the standard swimming cap. Then, about the time I'm wondering how the stylist is going to color my hair if it's all underneath this torturous cap, she picks up a tiny, mean-looking crochet hook. I know my eyes got as big as saucers. The beautician takes that hook and starts poking pin-sized holes into the rubber cap and pulling comparably sized small strands of my hair through the holes. She's talking ninety to nothing to the other beauticians and piercing my very tender head with that sharp weapon, um instrument, at the same breakneck speed. By the time she has pulled all of my hair out of the extremely tight cap I look like a damaged Barbie doll head and I'm crying. Of course, when the clueless stylist pops her gum and asks me, "Honey, you ok?" I lie and say I'm fine. That ladies, is what I've gone through to be beautiful. Now, like I said, you go back to that previous question, 'fess up and put something on those lines! Otherwise I'm going to feel pretty foolish.

Truthfully, there's nothing unbiblical about doing what we can, within reason, to look our best and put our daintiest foot forward. But our cultural has sold many of us a pretty pink shopping bag full of lies and, instead of returning them for a refund, we keep going back to the same deceptive sources for some more. Today I'm challenging you to go get that pretty pink bag, take all those lies out, lay them on the table before you, and join me in examining them for what they are. Let's get to the truth about beauty before our attempts to keep up with our culture absolutely kill us.

While this may not seem like a life and death matter that warrants a lesson in a biblical worldview study, we actually do need to see what the Bible has to say about beauty, where it comes from, how we get it, and how we measure it. Just ask those who have lost loved ones to eating disorders, plastic surgeries gone bad, diet pill fiascos, or suicide if beauty isn't a life and death issue. If you're the mother of a young girl, you need to gird yourself with some sound, biblical reasoning so you can teach your daughter how to be truly beautiful inside and out. You'll need to know what worldly beauty advice is potentially sending her over the edge and you'll need to be equipped to go to battle for her assessment of true beauty. And if you're the mother of a son, you need to know what kind of beauty the Bible describes as truly desirous and what kind it warns against seeking out and linking up with. Ladies, the world's exploitation of beauty sells magazines, movies, cars and toothpaste. And we're the ones paying the price.

In order to make sure we get a balanced perspective on what the Bible has to say about beauty, I'm going to have you look up a good number of scriptures. Beside the scripture reference, I'll supply two statements that could reflect the teaching you find there. Put a check mark beside the accurate, biblical statement. Leave the false statement blank.

1 Peter 3:3   ____ You should *never* wear jewelry, do your hair, or wear fine clothes.

____ Your beauty should not consist *merely* of wearing jewelry, doing your hair, or wearing fine clothes.

1 Peter 3:4   ____ A gentle and quiet spirit makes you a stand-out beauty in God's eyes.

____ A gentle and quiet spirit will make you invisible and mousy.

1 Peter 3:5   ____ A gentle and quiet spirit actually adorns your external features.

____ A gentle and quiet spirit makes you seem old and old-fashioned.

Psalm 139:14   ____ I am created uniquely and wonderfully by a loving and creative God.

____ I am a random combination of my dad's big nose and my mom's pear-shaped build.

Proverbs 31:30   ____ A woman who has a charming form and beauty deserves our praise.

____ A woman who fears the Lord earns the admiration of others.

1 Cor. 6:19-20   ____ My body is a temple for God's Spirit and I should care for and decorate it accordingly.

____ My body is mine to care for and decorate just as I choose.

Colossians 3:1-5   ____ Spending a lot of time, money and energy on our appearance is a noble and worthy pursuit.

____ Spending a lot of time and energy pursuing the things above is a noble and worthy pursuit.

1 Tim. 2:9-10   ____ The Bible provides the standard for how I am to clothe my body.

____ I can wear whatever is in fashion and whatever conveys my personality.

Proverbs 31:22   _____   I should only wear clothing that helps me blend in, nothing colorful or trendy.

_____   I can wear fashionable, trendy clothing that speaks well of *whose* I am.

While the Bible does not have a vast amount to say specifically about beauty, it does address the emphasis we should or should not place on physical beauty. First Peter 3 indicates that while it is acceptable to wear jewelry, arrange our hair stylishly, and dress fashionably, our greater attention should be given to developing inner beauty. Quite honestly, that just doesn't sound like as much fun to most of us. Who ever heard of having a day of *inner* beauty at the spa? And there are no cosmetics we can sample and play with that give our hearts a lovely, wholesome glow. But diligently pursuing a gentle and quiet spirit—two of the qualities of inner beauty—results in a loveliness that permeates the entire being of a woman, and even radiates from her countenance. Inner beauty brightens the eyes, turns up the corners of the mouth, puts a song-like quality in the voice, and infuses a woman's posture with dignity and grace.

Think about a godly woman you know who epitomizes this biblical brand of beauty. Perhaps she is an older woman whose head is crowned with gray hair and whose eyes are framed by laugh lines. Perhaps she is a middle-aged woman who carries herself with grace and dignity even though her school-aged kids demand much of her. Or she could be a young woman who looks to the future with hope and bright-eyed faith. Go ahead. Don't be hesitant to name someone. It's an honor. Writer her name on the line below and detail what makes her so beautiful in your eyes.

_____

_____

_____

_____

_____

Godly beauty, the kind the Bible encourages us to seek, is available to every woman who is willing to submit to the loving and skillful hand of the Creator. He will chisel away that which is ugly, self-centered, brash, offensive, and harmful to others. He will soften the rough edges, heal any festering wounds, polish the positive qualities to a holy glow, highlight that which reflects His own glorious character, and fit you with a timeless wardrobe of love, joy, peace, patience, kindness, goodness, gentleness, faithfulness, and self-control. Talk about lovely.

Not only is biblical beauty attainable; it is the only beauty that is true and lasting. Because we live in a fallen world, our adult bodies are always in the process of decaying, little by little. I know that's an ugly thought, but it's true. While we certainly need to take the best care of our bodies that we possibly can, we don't need to obsess about trying to hold on to that which no longer is. There is no shame in aging, especially if we do it gracefully and faithfully. And when we invest in that which gives us godly, inner beauty we can be assured of future returns. Unlike physical glamour, inner beauty does not fade, but only grows more alluring with time.

Finally, godly beauty actually is also the deepest form of beauty. It is not shallow, skin deep, superficial, or digitally enhanced. It's the real thing and the most completely transforming. Consider the fact that every time you even look at a cover of a fashion or women's magazine you are seeing an elusive deception. The model or celebrity on that cover probably has a personal trainer with whom she works out religiously and thoroughly. Because her body and face are her most marketable assets, she invests large sums of money in a plethora of procedures that keep her skin flawless, her teeth sparkling, her hair healthy, and her body toned and slim. The day of the photo shoot that model has professionals on hand to do her hair, makeup, and nails. She is dressed by a professional stylist and photographed by a topnotch photographer. And even then, when the photo is developed, her image is digitally enhanced to improve her skin tone, the brightness of her teeth and eyes, the size of her thighs, the curve of her waist, and the length of her nails. Beautiful? Yes. Deceptive? Absolutely. "Charm is deceitful and beauty is vain." (Proverbs 31:30a) But when our faces glow with a confidence in our Lord, our eyes sparkle with a seasoned joy, and our bodies are clothed with grace and dignity, there is no deception involved. That's real beauty and it permeates from deep within.

For a glimpse at a woman who exhibited both physical beauty and inner, godly beauty, let's take a quick look at Esther. I take us to this passage just before we complete our study because I want us to see the positive outcome of developing a godly, gentle and quiet spirit. I want us to see that regardless of how beautiful we may or may not be on the outside, inner beauty is so powerful that it can literally move the heart of a king and, indeed, the heart of a nation.

At the point where we will pick up with our reading in the book of Esther, this young Jewish girl is being taken to the palace of King Ahasuerus to join his royal harem. She is one of many young virgins from which the king will choose his new queen. Please read Esther 2:8-17. As you read, circle, if you will, the words "found favor" or "won …favor" or "pleased" every time you see them. Answer the following questions based on this passage.

Whose favor does Esther win in verse 9 (refer to verse 8)? _____

What was the result of her finding such favor? _____

_____

According to verse 12, what kind of preparation did Esther and all the other women

receive before seeing the king? _____

_____

Whose favor does Esther win in verse 15? _____

How does verse 17 describe the king's reaction to Esther? _____

_____

Now let's think through this a bit. In this passage we learn that Esther is obviously a beautiful young woman. That is the very reason she was chosen to be in the harem after all. But Esther is more than just candy for the eyes. She has something within her that causes her to rise to the top of everyone's list of favorites. She is the favorite of Hegai, the chief custodian of all these young women who are receiving constant beauty treatments. Eventually she is chosen by the king to be his new bride, not just because she's beautiful to look at, but because he *loves* her. But perhaps most interestingly, Esther also earns the admiration and favor of all the other young virgins. Think on that one a minute. Have you ever been a part of a pageant or beauty contest? Have you ever even been in a room filled with teenaged girls who are vying for any attention at all? Think suspicious eyes, cat claws coming out, whispers behind the back, and big green fits of jealousy. Women who are in competition with one another for any type of distinction usually do not develop deep fondness for each other. But these women, all of which were groomed and pampered for the express purpose of winning the king's heart, felt favorably toward Esther, according to Esther 2:15. *That* is some kind of beauty! They all had outer beauty, but Esther had an inner quality that gained her the favor of all who knew her, and it caused her to stand out to everyone who encountered her.

Looking Out From My Front Porch
We face a constant barrage of deceptive messages about beauty in this culture. Every time I buy groceries I am challenged by the magazine covers at the checkout counter to lose weight, tone up, change my hairstyle, use collagen, get breast implants, whiten my teeth, or buy a new outfit. The longer I gaze upon these digitally enhanced photos, the less content I feel with my own "fearfully and wonderfully made" body. If I read the captions on the magazine covers I am lured into believing that my life measures up poorly in comparison to the lives of the beautiful people of this world.

I don't know about you, but now in my 40s I still have to consciously battle against the lies of my culture to keep from losing what self-esteem I do have. I have to stare those glossy pictures down and remind myself they are a big lie, a worldly deception. It's a war that plays out in my mind almost every time I am confronted with the world's view of beauty. But I am determined that the way to win this war is not to engage in the world's game of accumulating multiple beauty products, trying every beauty treatment imaginable, and beating myself up over every distinguishing flaw or sign of aging. Instead I will win this war by turning my attention to developing the inner beauty spoken of in 1 Peter 3. That is where I will devote my energy, time, and money so I can develop a beauty that goes beyond lipstick.

Let's do a little self-evaluation to see if we have a biblical view of beauty or if we have bought into the current worldview of what is beautiful. Below each question I've inserted a scale for you to rate whether or not your views and your behavior in that particular area indicate that you have a worldly perception of beauty or a biblical understanding of and approach to beauty.

1. Do I spend more time each day on my physical appearance than I do in prayer, Bible study, or worship?

   Worldly   Biblical

2. Am I exercising feverishly to lose weight in order to gain the approval of others or do I want to be self-disciplined with my body so that it honors God?

   Worldly   Biblical

3. Do I spend excessive money on makeup, hair products, clothes, cosmetic procedures or exercise equipment, or do I spend an amount that is God-honoring?

Worldly   Biblical

4. Am I obsessing over what I eat in an effort to be fashionably thin or do I try to eat in a healthy way so I can better serve God?

Worldly   Biblical

5. Is there anything about my physical appearance that I obsess over and wish I could change, or does "my soul know very well" that I am fearfully and wonderfully made?

Worldly   Biblical

6. Am I jealous of the physical appearance of others or am I content with my own features and glad for women who are blessed with physical beauty?

Worldly   Biblical

7. Do I wear clothing that shows off my body and deliberately draws the attention of men or do I purchase and wear clothing that suits my personality and body shape, but is also modest and honorable?

Worldly   Biblical

8. When I'm at a public event, do I compare my appearance to the appearance of others or do I seek out people to be kind and loving to?

Worldly   Biblical

9. Do I choose my friends based on their appearance or do I look for friends who have inner beauty that reflects the glory of God?

Worldly   Biblical

10. Am I teaching my daughter or granddaughter that inner beauty can move the hearts of people or am I developing in her a drive to be physically beautiful at all cost?

Worldly   Biblical

Leaving My Front Porch

Perhaps no other topic we've covered has such personal implications for us women. The truth is that most women struggle with some sort of self-esteem issues, and usually these issues are rooted in a desire for someone to think we are beautiful. Dear friend, your God thinks you are gorgeous. He is stunned by your beauty. And the more your inner beauty develops, the more He will cause that loveliness to surface in your countenance. Thank Him today for making you beautiful, unique, and full of potential. Praise Him for a job well done!

Some Final Thoughts

As we bring this Bible study on developing a Christian worldview to a close, I want to thank you for taking this journey with me. You have honored me by reading my words, by considering my thoughts. But I hope the journey has meant more to you than an opportunity to see what I have to say on some current topics. I hope you, like me, have taken an honest look at your current worldview, honestly evaluating how it was shaped. I also hope you have earnestly applied the biblical concepts we discussed for reformulating our worldview based on a healthy fear of our God and a genuine respect for His Word. I know I will continue to be challenged to take in the information overload I encounter each day, sift it through the character of God and the precepts of His Word, and maintain a biblical view of my world. Let's covenant to help each other stick close to our biblical foundation as we continue our pilgrimage through this very strange and worldly land.

Finally, ladies, I've enjoyed our investigation into biblical womanhood. There is so much more we could have studied in this area, but I am confident we now have a good foundation under our dainty little belts. Isn't it grand being a woman? Yes, it's hard and complicated in our current culture, but it's also downright fun. Let's celebrate our femininity in a way that honors God and builds up the body of Christ. And don't forget to treat yourself to that much deserved pedicure. You've earned it!

God bless you!

Kay

---

[1] *The Words of John Adams, Second President of the United States: With a Life of the Author, Notes and Illustrations, by His Grandson Charles Francis Adams,* Vol. III (Boston: Charles C. Little and James Brown, 1851), 171.

[2] Nancy Leigh DeMoss, editor, *Biblical Womanhood in the Home,* (Wheaton, IL: Crossway Books, 2002), back cover.

[3] John Piper and Wayne Grudem, editors, *Recovering Biblical Manhood & Womanhood: A Response to Evangelical Feminism* (Wheaton, IL: Crossway Books, 1991), 36.

[4] Barbara Hughes, *Disciplines of a Godly Woman,* (Wheaton, IL: Crossway books, 2001).

[5] Carolyn Mahaney, contributor, *Biblical Womanhood in the Home,* (Wheaton, IL: Crossway Books, 2002), 30-31.

[6] http://www.redorbit.com/news/health/394249/new_data_suggest_that_some_increased_infertility_attributed_to_environmental/

[7] http://www.cnn.com/2006/HEALTH/parenting/05/08/mothers.index/

[8] http://www.nytimes.com/2008/10/16/health/16infant.html

[9] Robin Marantz Henig, "The Price of Perfection," *The Journal of Biblical Counseling,* Volume 15, Number 2, Winter 1997, 34-38. The article originally appeared in the May/June 1996 issue of *Civilization* and was reprinted with permission.

Discussion Questions

1. What are some ways men and women are generally different? How does our world view those differences?

2. In your estimation is it important for women to nurture their feminine side? Is it important for women to act like women, at least to some degree? Why or why not? What are the spiritual implications of women behaving in a feminine way and men being masculine?

3. What do you find confusing about being a woman in today's culture, if anything?

4. Why does a woman's help make a difference in a man's life? Conversely, what are some of the things women do that *do not* help men?

5. What are some of the ways the Proverbs 31 woman nurtures her children? Since she seems to juggle a lot, what does the passage indicate she does in order to make her children a priority? What are some of the things that get in your way of nurturing your children?

6. Have you had an older woman nurture you as a mentor? How did that relationship benefit you?

7. Why do you think it's important to be a good keeper of the home? How can we pass this skill and role down to our daughters effectively?

8. If pretty eyes, silky hair, a trim figure and manicured nails are characteristics of physical beauty, what are some traits of the deeper, inner beauty spoken of in the Bible? How do these traits show up on the outside, or do they?

Made in the USA
Las Vegas, NV
27 March 2021